Lake Geneva / Lac Leman
Global Connections

Copyright © 2024 by Mel Swain

The right of Mel Swain to be identified as author of this work has been asserted by him in accordance with the Copyright, Designs and Patents Act 1988.

All rights reserved. No part of this book may be reproduced or used in any manner without written permission of the copyright owner, except for the use of quotations in a book review. This work must not be narrated by artificial intelligence or other non-human narrator without the author's prior and express written consent.

ISBN: 978-1-80541-625-8 paperback
ISBN: 978-1-80541-624-1 ebook

Mel was born and raised in Gillingham in the United Kingdom. An Open University graduate who trained as a teacher in Brighton, he has lived in West Sussex ever since and taught in four comprehensive schools. Author of 'The Medway and the Military'.

Lake Geneva / Lac Leman Global Connections

Mel Swain

Contents

1   **Around The Lake In 180 Minutes**   1
*An outline of the lake's main features,
towns and villages*

2   **Money, Money, Money**   9
*World Economic Forum – Patek Philippe –
Coco Chanel*

3   **If Music Be The Food Of Love**   17
*Stravinsky – Tchaikovsky – Clara Haskil –
music festivals*

4   **'Now You Has Jazz'**   23
*Claude Nobs – Montreux Jazz Festival –
Freddie Mercury – Shania Twain*

5   **Man's Humanity To Man And Nature**   29
*Red Cross – Geneva Conventions –
World Health Organisation – WWF – UNICEF*

6   **The UNICEF Connection**   37
*Goodwill ambassadors – Audrey Hepburn –
Peter Ustinov*

7   **To Believe Or Not To Believe**   45
Calvin – Dostoevsky – Rousseau – Voltaire

8   **Scientific Connections**   53
*Religion v. science – Henri Nestle – chocolate –
CERN – Large Hadron Collider*

9	**Life, Death And Politics**	61
	Gandhi – Rolland – Nehru – Charlie Chaplin –	
	Leon Gambetta – Edmund Ludlow – Empress Sisi	
10	**War And Peace**	71
	Treaties of Lausanne – Versailles 1919 – League of	
	Nations – Montreux Convention 1936	
11	**From Russia With Love Stories**	77
	Leo Tolstoy - Vladimir Nabokov	
12	**Anglo-American Literary Connections**	83
	Henry James – Ernest Hemingway – Noel Coward –	
	Graham Greene	
13	**Medieval Connections**	95
	Shelley – Byron – Chillon – Bonivard –	
	House of Savoy – Morges castle – Yvoire	
14	**Take The Water Or The Wine**	99
	Evian – Lake Geneva vineyards – Fete des	
	Vignerons – Vevey Alimentarium	
15	**A Healthy Body**	105
	Pierre de Coubertin – IOC – UEFA – Swiss	
	Museum of Games – SNG - Bol d'Or Mirabaud	
Miscellaneous		115

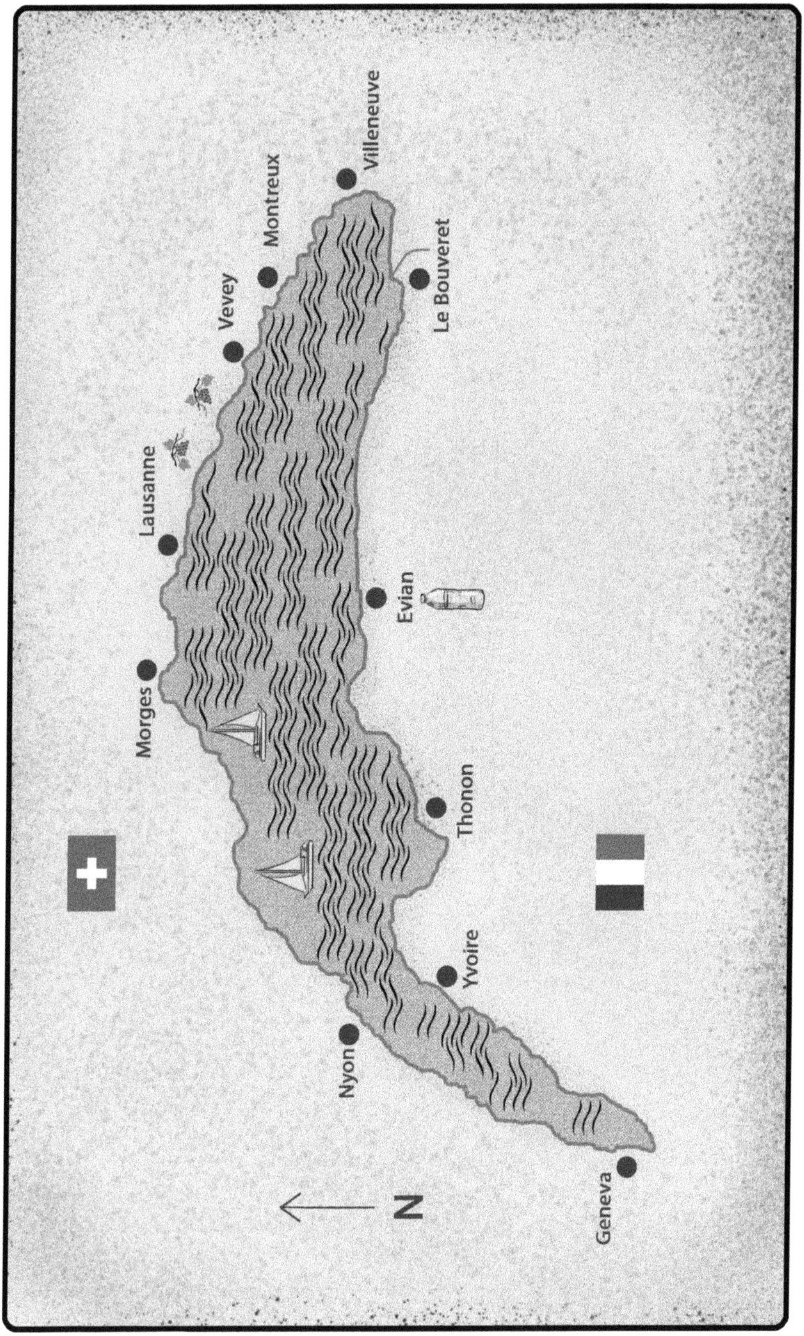
Villeneuve
Montreux
Le Bouveret
Vevey
Lausanne
Evian
Morges
Thonon
Yvoire
Nyon
Geneva
N

Chapter 1

Around The Lake In 180 Minutes

"I love the region around Lake Geneva. The landscape is beautiful, very peaceful, and such a nice place to relax and spend time outdoors. It's always a pleasure to come back home."

Stan Wawrinka, tennis player

Switzerland is a landlocked country but it does have approximately 7,000 lakes. The biggest lake which is completely within the country is Lake Neuchatel, but Lake Geneva (59% in Switzerland and 41% in France) is even bigger and is the largest lake in Western Europe. It is formed by the River Rhone, which enters the lake from the east near Villeneuve. It leaves the lake at the western end through the city of Geneva, where it is joined by the River Arve before running through South-East France to the Mediterranean Sea.

Lake Geneva is nearly 73 km (45 miles) long, and its maximum width is 13 km (8 miles) between Lausanne and Evian. The average depth of the lake is 154.4 metres (507 feet), and the deepest point is 310 metres (1,020 feet). When viewed from above, the shape of the lake is similar to a shark or a crescent moon. The lake is actually tidal, but not that anyone would notice, since the variation is only four millimetres. Geologists have proved that a tsunami shook the lake in the year 563, causing extensive damage with waves of up to 13 metres high. It occurred after a whole face of a mountain collapsed and was followed by an earth tremor.

Switzerland has four national languages, but Lake Geneva is entirely situated within the French-speaking part, where it is known as Lac Leman. German speakers are likely to refer to it as Genfersee, while Italian speakers call it either Lago Lemano or Lago di Ginevra. The lake is surrounded by four Swiss cantons – Geneva, Vaud, Valais and Fribourg – and two French departments (Ain and Haute-Savoie).

In 1823, Edward Church, an American businessman and the US Consul in France, launched pleasure cruises on Lake Geneva. He was inspired by the steamboats that travelled along the Hudson River, and his 'Guillaume Tell' paddle steamer operated along the northern shoreline from Geneva to Ouchy. Nowadays boats on the lake are operated by Compagnie Generale de Navigation sur le Lac Leman (CGN), which was created in 1873. In 2024, CGN had a total of 19 vessels, which is believed to be the world's largest fleet of steamboats, eight of which are Belle Epoque paddle steamers. Geneva is the home port for eight of CGN's fleet.

Lake Geneva has more than 20 indigenous species of fishes, and a few more were introduced in the 19th century. In 1827, it became the first place for the speed of sound to be tested in freshwater.

This isn't another tourist guide; the focus of this book is on the many connections between Lake Geneva and the rest of the world. However, it might assist those who are not familiar with the lake if a brief sketch of the significant towns and villages on its shores is provided. It takes around three hours to drive around the whole lake, and we'll start our circuit in Geneva and head around the northern shore.

Geneva is the second largest city in Switzerland (after Zurich) with a population in 2023 of 633,000. People originally settled there because of its strategic position at the south-western end of the lake, where there's a shallow crossing point of the River Rhone. The long and busy Mont Blanc Bridge connects the two halves of the city. Geneva is famous for its 147-metre high fountain known as the Jet d'Eau, dating from 1951, which shoots up water at a speed of 200 km (125 miles) an hour; at any time seven tonnes of water are in the air. The highest point of the old town on the south bank has been a place of worship since pagan days, but the present Cathedrale St-Pierre was begun in the 12th century.

The medieval town of Coppet has a number of thick-walled stone houses and other architectural treasures.

The chateau in the town was bought in 1784 by Necker, Louis XVI's finance minister. His daughter Germaine de Staël, the main opponent of Napoleon, used to invite the European intellectual elite of the early 19th century there to what became the 'Salon de l'Europe'.

Nyon is dominated by a fairy-tale castle, and it hosts a number of annual festivals and events. The town was once a Roman outpost, and there is a Roman mosaic in the courtyard of the castle's museum. Nyon is the home of the Leman Museum, which focuses on all aspects of nature and life relating to the lake, and a chateau just outside of the town houses the Swiss National Museum. Another chateau, which houses the Vaud Military Museum, can be found at the port of Morges; a tulip festival takes place in the adjacent garden every spring. The town also has a museum named after Alexis Forel, the Swiss engraver and artist. From Morges there is the best view on the entire lake of Mont Blanc, Europe's highest mountain.

9.5 km (6 miles) to the east of Morges, and 62 km (38.5 miles) north east of Geneva, is Lau-sanne, the capital of the canton of Vaud. It is a business, administrative and university centre, situated on a steep hillside, with a population in 2023 of about 460,000. The city has 46 buildings or sites which are listed as Swiss heritage sites of national significance. Its Gothic cathedral was consecrated by Pope Gregory X in 1275. The year 1861 saw the inauguration of the railway that leads eastwards from Lausanne through the Rhone Valley to the Simplon Pass, connecting Switzerland with Italy.

On the lakeside just to the south of Lausanne is Ouchy, which was once a fishing village. It was incorporated into the city of Lausanne in the mid-19th century to serve as a port. A few kilometres to the east is the medieval village of Lutry, which was founded by monks in the 11th century.

The beautiful resort of Vevey, where milk chocolate was invented, has an unusually large market square close to the lake. Over a long weekend every August, the town hosts its International Street Artists Festival, which attracts acrobats, clowns, jugglers and mime artists from across the world. In 1861, the French novelist Victor Hugo stopped at Vevey and sent a letter to a friend describing his appreciation of the cleanliness and the mild climate of the town. On the slopes to the north of Vevey are the famous Lavaux vineyards. In nearby La Tour-de-Peilz, the 13th century castle, which overlooks a small yacht harbour, houses the Swiss Museum of Games.

By the time that Montreux is reached, the lake has narrowed and steep mountains shelter the town from north-easterly winds. The town is a full-time international tourist resort which holds numerous events, including conferences, TV awards, art exhibitions, and jazz and classical music festivals. Clarens is the largest and most populated neighbourhood in the municipality. Jutting into the water just beyond Montreux is Chillon, a castle which is over 900 years old; it is the foremost tourist attraction on Lake Geneva and the most visited historical monument in Switzerland. From the Port du Basset at the western end of Montreux, there is an 8 km (5 miles) lakeside walk to Villeneuve, a small town at the eastern end of the lake. Villeneuve was founded by Thomas of Savoy in 1214 on the site of earlier Celtic and Roman settlements.

Le Bouveret has a water amusement park which is open all year round, along with a hospitality school, but it is most famous for its 20,000 square metres Swiss Vapeur Parc. It is entirely dedicated to miniature trains, installations and works of art, such as the replica of the George Washington Bridge in New York, which was built to scale. After crossing the border into France, the first place of note will be the spa town of Evian, which features later in this book. As our journey continues, Thonon, a historical town and thermal resort, will be reached. The town has an open-air fishing and lake museum and is also the location of the Chateau de Ripaille, the former residence of the Dukes of Savoy.

Close by and 24 km (15 miles) from Geneva, is the medieval village of Yvoire, considered to be one of the most beautiful villages in France. Then finally we're back in Geneva, the city which the American historian Lewis Mumford described as having "the sleepy tidiness of a man who combs his hair while still in his pyjamas". It is also a city which has a long history of banking and insurance, and it is the headquarters of, among many other organisations, the World Economic Forum.

Chapter 2

Money, Money, Money

"A United Nations study claims the happiest country in the world is Switzerland. When asked why they're so happy, Swiss people couldn't answer because their hands were counting money and their mouths were full of chocolate."

Conan O'Brien, American television host

There is a joke about an American who joins a queue in a Swiss bank with a suitcase full of money. When he reaches the counter, he says to the bank clerk in a hushed voice: "I've got a million dollars in this case". The clerk replies: "There's no need to whisper, sir, poverty is nothing to be ashamed of".

Switzerland has long been considered a safe and stable country in which to deposit money and where your financial privacy is protected. This is in no small part due to the country's constitutional principle of permanent neutrality. Switzerland doesn't get involved in overseas wars, but it does have a long humanitarian tradition, and it contributes generously to the foreign aid which is often required because of those conflicts. That long-established neutrality is a part of what makes Switzerland so distinct from its neighbouring countries; it has sometimes been described as an island surrounded by land.

Benefitting from its neutrality, during World War II Switzerland purchased large amounts of gold from both sides in the conflict. Other countries wanted Swiss francs because, apart from the American dollar, it was the only free convertible currency at the time. It is estimated that Swiss banks bought $1.7 billion worth of Nazi gold, including gold that had been plundered from the reserves of countries which Germany had overrun, especially Austria, Belgium, the Netherlands and Norway. Some of the gold had been confiscated from private individuals, or taken from the inmates of concentration camps. After the war, Switzerland agreed to pay reparations worth CHF 250 million, and to identify dormant accounts which were heirless.

Geneva's important role in global trading and banking (about 500 trading companies are based there) attracts talented people from all around the world. The city is currently home to 750 non-governmental organisations and 52 international organisations, one of which is the Intergovernmental Panel on Climate Change (IPCC), which made its headquarters there in 1988. About 32,000 international government officers live in and around the city.

Geneva was where the European Management Forum was established in 1971 by Klaus Schwab, a German engineer and economist, as a not-for-profit foundation.

Initially it focused on how European businesses could catch up with US management practices, but in 1987 it broadened its scope and became the World Economic Forum (WEF). Schwab was also professor of business policy at Geneva University from 1972 to 2003.

The mission statement of the WEF says it is "committed to improving the state of the world by engaging business, political, academic, and other leaders of society to shape global, regional, and industry agendas". It is best known for the annual gathering which, since 1974, has been held every January in the Swiss resort of Davos. It is attended by many business leaders and politicians to consider the major global issues of the day (and maybe to get in some skiing). The annual meeting gradually expanded its focus from management to economic and social issues.

'Stakeholder capitalism' is a concept that Schwab has promoted for decades and which has been prominent in the WEF's 'Great Reset' plan since June 2020. The idea is that global capitalism should be transformed so that corporations no longer focus solely on serving shareholders, but become custodians of society by creating value for customers, suppliers, employees, communities and other 'stakeholders'. The way the WEF sees stakeholder capitalism being carried out is through a range of 'multi-stakeholder partnerships', bringing together the private sector, governments and civil society across all areas of global governance. In May 2024, Schwab announced that he would be standing down as the executive chairman of the WEF at the end of the year.

The WEF attracts criticism from those who see its January jaunt as merely a gathering of the wealthy and privileged. It is argued that those who own most of the world's resources discuss how to arrange governance for the world economy more or less on the basis of what they think is right. The WEF's member organisations are nearly all transnational corporations with annual turnovers of billions of dollars. The forum is seen by many as an instrument for political and business leaders to take decisions without having to account to their electorate or shareholders. When US president Bill Clinton spoke at Davos in 2000 he pleaded: "Globalisation will and must march on, but in future don't leave the little guy out. Globalisation is about more than markets alone; it means interdependence, which means none of us who are fortunate can any longer help ourselves unless we are prepared to help our neighbours."

At the WEF gathering in Davos in 2020, a stainless steel Patek Philippe Aquanaut on a rubber strap adorned the wrist of the chief executive officer of Lloyds Banking Group, but it probably wasn't the only watch of that brand being worn in the meeting. Patek Philippe is a Swiss luxury watch and clock producer based in Geneva. It is one of the oldest watch manufacturers in the world and was established in 1839 by Antoni Patek and Adrien Philippe.

It had been Huguenot refugees in the late 16th century whose technical expertise had started the development of Swiss watch-making. Geneva at that time was effectively a theocracy (a state governed by religious law), and watches were the only jewellery allowed under the strict religious ordinances. Geneva was the location of the first guild of watch-makers in the early 17th century.

Cuckoo clocks were developed in the Black Forest area of Germany in the early 18th century, and later they were imported into Switzerland and sold in tourist shops. However, it was in 1845 that the first machines capable of producing identical parts were invented, which then led to mass-production and changed watch craftsmanship into an industry. Since the mid-19th century, Geneva and the surrounding areas have never ceased producing timepieces, and every April the city hosts its Watches and Wonders Exhibition; in 2023 it attracted 48 exhibitors and 43,000 visitors from 125 different countries. It is hardly surprising that Switzerland has sometimes been nicknamed "the land of cuckoo clocks and watches".

At the Great Exhibition in London in 1851, Queen Victoria acquired a keyless pendant watch and had another exclusive Patek Philippe timepiece for wearing pinned to clothing. Women wore watches on their wrists long before men, and it was Patek Philippe which made the first Swiss wristwatch in Geneva in 1868, after it had been commissioned by the Countess Koscowicz of Hungary.

Patek Philippe timepieces have always fetched high prices in auctions worldwide, and the company has used the slogan: "You never actually own a Patek Philippe; you merely look after it for the next generation". In 2014, the company created the Grandmaster Chime Ref. 5175, which is one of the world's most complicated wristwatches. There has been a Patek Philippe Museum in Geneva since 2001.

Another company active in watch making, as well as aerospace markets, is Del West, which was founded by Alfred Sommer in 1973 in Roche, a municipality in the canton of Vaud. This company is a world leader in materials processing for the Formula One business; it has three sites in the US and employs nearly 300 people in 30 different trades.

What goes with jewellery and expensive watches better than designer clothes and perfume? Gabrielle Bonheur Chanel, who gained her nickname 'Coco' during her time as a cafe singer, was a French fashion designer and businesswoman. She was born into poverty in Saumur in 1883, and after her mother died, her father left her in an orphanage, where nuns taught her to sew. Chanel started out designing and selling hats, opening her first shop in 1910. She used knitted jersey to create her first collections, and she once said "my fortune is built on that old jersey that I'd put on because it was cold in Deauville".

That wasn't true. Her fortune was based on her 'little black dress' and the perfume Chanel No 5. By 1920 she was promoting the colour black as a stylish and versatile choice for women's wardrobes. Soon that dress, which became known as LBD and was on the cover of 'Vogue' magazine in 1926, was a global hit. Chanel herself reminded people that "fashion is made to become unfashionable", but her LBD remained popular during the 1930s, partly because of its simplicity and affordability.

When she introduced No 5 in May 1921, Chanel became the first major fashion designer to market a perfume. It was created by Ernest Beaux, who had previously supplied the Russian imperial court, and he used over 80 ingredients, including jasmine and sandalwood. He initially produced ten samples and Chanel chose number five, which was her favourite number. A later perfume was called Chanel No 19 because she had been born on 19th August. Many years later, an LBD perfume (La Petite Robe Noire) was launched by the French company Guerlain, firstly as a limited edition in 2009 and 2011 and then to a broad market in 2012.

When the Second World War began in 1939, the House of Chanel in Paris closed. When the city was liberated from the Nazis in August 1944, Chanel was arrested because of her German associations during the war and the suspicion that she was a Nazi spy. Following her surprise release in 1945, she followed her lover, Hans Gunther von Dincklage, who had been director of propaganda for the Third Reich, to Switzerland, where they lived together near Lausanne until 1954.

Why was Chanel allowed to escape justice? Having friends in high places seems to be the most likely explanation. Perhaps her former lover, the Duke of Westminster, intervened on her behalf. We do know that British prime minister Winston Churchill was concerned that she might be forced to testify about her activities in a trial. He feared that she would expose the pro-Nazi sympathies and activities of some top-level British officials, members of society, and at least one member of the royal family.

In 1954, at the age of 71, Chanel said that she "was dying of boredom" and felt that her days as a fashion designer were not yet over, so she moved back to Paris and put on a new show later that year. She died in Paris in 1971, but she is buried in the Bois-de-Vaux, the main cemetery of Lausanne.

Chapter 3

If Music Be The Food Of Love

"Music is the heart of life. She speaks love. Without it there is no possible good, and with it everything is beautiful."

Franz Liszt, Hungarian composer

In 2002, the British writer Chris Greenhalgh published a novel entitled 'Coco and Igor'. In 2009, it was adapted for the film 'Coco Chanel and Igor Stravinsky', which was released in France and starred Anna Mouglalis as Chanel and Mads Mikkelsen as Stravinsky. The film is based on the short-lived affair which they had in 1920-21.

Igor Stravinsky was a controversial Russian composer who was born in 1882. He was particularly famous for 'The Firebird', a ballet and orchestral concert work, and for 'The Rite of Spring'. In 1910, Stravinsky decided that his wife and family would spend their summers in Russia and their winters on Lake Geneva, where the microclimate was considered beneficial for his wife's health. For five winters they made their home in Clarens, where Stravinsky composed part of 'The Rite of Spring', and then in 1915 they lived at three different addresses in Morges.

'The Rite of Spring' was ill-received at its premiere in Paris in 1913. Its original choreography was by the Russian ballet dancer Vaslav Nijinsky, and it depicts various pagan rituals celebrating the advent of spring, after which a young girl is chosen as a sacrificial victim to dance herself to death. The French composer Claude Debussy praised Stravinsky for "having enlarged the boundaries of the permissible" in music.

Unlike most of the audience at its premiere, Coco Chanel was impressed by 'The Rite of Spring'. When she was introduced to Stravinsky in the spring of 1920, she invited him to bring his family and stay in her villa. They had been forced to flee Russia after the revolution of 1917, and Stravinsky had acquired French nationality. When they were staying with her, Chanel had an affair with Stravinsky, something which his estate still tries to deny. However, Chanel gave details of it to her biographer Paul Morand in 1946, and the Chanel label supported the making of the 2009 film.

Stravinsky eventually settled in the US and became an American citizen; he died in New York in 1971. A concert hall, the Auditorium Stravinsky, was opened in Montreux in 1973 in his honour. It has exceptional acoustics (which cost CHF 7 million), was built to accommodate 4,000 people, and is one of the best equipped concert halls in Europe. In 1985, a road in Clarens was named Rue du Sacre du Printemps (Rite of Spring Street).

An earlier Russian composer who stayed in Clarens three

times between 1877 and 1879 was Pyotr Ilyich Tchaikovsky. He was born in May 1840 in Votkinsk, a small town not far from the Ural Mountains, and he started composing when he was just four years old. Apparently he enjoyed picking mushrooms! He spent three years as a civil servant before enrolling at the St Petersburg Conservatory in 1862. At first he wanted to be a conductor as well as a composer, but he had a weird belief that his head might roll off when he was conducting. That caused him to clutch his chin with his left hand while trying to lead the orchestra. He graduated in 1865, but not as a conductor.

Tchaikovsky was gay, and his first love was Sergey Kireyev, a fellow student. Excerpts from his letters, which reveal his sexual preferences, have been censored in Russia. He felt compelled by societal pressures to seek a wife, and in 1877 he married a former student. Not surprisingly, the marriage was a disaster, and the couple only lived together for ten weeks. It was then that Tchaikovsky went on his travels and stayed in Clarens, where he wrote a violin concerto and worked on his opera 'Eugene Onegin'.

Tchaikovsky was the first Russian composer whose music would make a lasting impression internationally. He was a big fan of Shakespeare, which would account for his 'Romeo and Juliet Overture'. He was particularly famous for his ballets 'Swan Lake' and 'The Nutcracker', the '1812 Overture', and the first of his three piano concertos. In

1877, Tchaikovsky occupied the Villa Richelieu on the site of what is now the Hotel Royal Plaza in Montreux; the villa was later turned into a hotel and then demolished in 1970. He also visited Geneva on six occasions between 1873 and 1889.

Tchaikovsky died in St Petersburg in November 1893. There is some mystery about the cause of his death, although it is usually attributed to cholera arising from drinking unboiled water at a restaurant. There has been speculation that he killed himself, either with poison or by contracting cholera intentionally. Not long before his death, Cambridge University awarded him an honorary doctor of music degree.

A biography by music professor Simon Morrison, published in August 2024, contradicts previous gloomy accounts of Tchaikovsky's personality, describing him as "a fun-loving man with a 'Monty Python' sense of humour". His life was the subject of a 1971 film, 'The Music Lovers', starring Richard Chamberlain and Glenda Jackson.

The Montreux area seems to have been a favourite place for East European musicians. Clara Haskil was a Jewish girl who was born in Romania in 1895. As a small child she suffered from pneumonia, and then she spent four of her teenage years in a nursing home in plaster because of curvature of the spine. She also had a tumour on her optic nerve, and both conditions left her in constant pain throughout her life. Yet by the age of five, she was already an impressive pianist. When she was seven, her uncle took her to Vienna, where she also learned to play the violin. However, her tutor recommended her to the Paris Conservatoire, which she entered at the age of ten, after which she concentrated on her piano playing.

The German invasion of France in World War II forced Haskil to flee from Paris to Marseilles, which was in the unoccupied part of the country. After she moved to Vevey in 1951, the French government awarded her the Legion d'Honneur. She eventually settled near Chamby, a hamlet within the municipality of Montreux. She died suddenly in 1960 after a fall in a railway station in Brussels. In 1962, a road in Vevey where she once lived was renamed Rue Clara Haskil.

As a mark of their love for her and her music, Haskil's friends founded an association in her memory, and every two years the Clara Haskil International Piano Competition is organised. The first competitions were held in Lucerne, but since 1973 they have been held in Vevey. The purpose of each competition is to discover a young musician capable of representing the values of musicality, sensitivity, humility, constant re-evaluation and continual striving for excellence. The organisers only award one Clara Haskil Prize, which cannot be shared, and the jury may decide not to award the prize at all. The winner receives CHF 25,000, and the other finalists each receive CHF 5,000.

That competition is part of the Festival of Montreux-Vevey. Among other events around the lake is an electronic music festival which has been held in Geneva in July in most years since 1997. An intimate jazz festival has taken place in Cully (a small village situated between Lutry and Vevey), much of it in cafes and wine cellars, every April since the 1980s. It usually last for nine days and includes composition workshops and a traditional children's concert; in 2023 it attracted 62,000 people. Nyon has hosted the Paleo Festival in late July every year since 1976, which started as a folk festival but has developed into a six-day event with over 250 shows across seven stages, covering an area of 84 hectares. Folk music remains its main focus, but it has gradually accommodated other genres and has become one of Europe's most important musical events. However, the Lake Geneva musical celebration which is world famous and attracts by far and away the most visitors is, of course, the Montreux Jazz Festival.

Chapter 4

'Now You Has Jazz'

That was a song written by the American composer Cole Porter for the 1956 film 'High Society'. The lyrics describe what instruments are needed to create jazz, a musical genre which, according to the American trumpeter and vocalist Louis Armstrong, "if you have to ask what it is, you'll never know". Jazz has been widely played and appreciated in Switzerland since the 1930s. However, what was needed before the second largest celebration of jazz in the world, after Montreal, was to become an annual feature was someone with the vision and dedication of Claude Nobs.

Nobs was born in Montreux in February 1936 and, after apprenticing as a cook, he worked in the local tourist office and began arranging concerts in 1964. One of his first concerts featured The Rolling Stones, but he said that he was forced to give away tickets because nobody had heard of them! In 1967, he organised the first Montreux Jazz Festival, which lasted for three days. It was an immediate success and became an annual event lasting for 16 days in the first half of July. It soon attracted stars such as Ella Fitzgerald and Miles Davis, and it expanded to incorporate rock and blues and other genres. In its

Chapter 4 - 'Now You Has Jazz'

history, the festival has seen performances from many famous artists, including Stevie Wonder, David Bowie, Aretha Franklin, Nina Simone, Bob Dylan, Led Zeppelin, Marvin Gaye, Prince, Elton John, Radiohead and Phil Collins. During the 1990s, Nobs shared the directorship of the festival with Quincy Jones and made Miles Davis an honorary host.

The Montreux Jazz Festival was originally held at the Montreux Casino. However, that venue burned down in December 1971 after an idiot in the audience fired a flare gun towards the ceiling during a Frank Zappa concert. Nobs, who had served as a volunteer fireman, saved several young people who had hidden in the casino thinking they would be sheltered from the flames. The English band Deep Purple, who had decided to produce an album in Montreux, were scheduled to record at the Montreux Casino. They went on to compose 'Smoke on the Water', a song about the fire in which they mention Nobs' bravery: "Funky Claude was running in and out, pulling kids out the ground". That song has been rated as one of the greatest guitar tracks of all time. Since 1973, the two main stages used for the festival have been the Auditorium Stravinsky and the Miles Davis Hall. Altogether 380 concerts are held, 250 of which are free, and the event attracts nearly 250,000 people each year.

On Christmas Eve 2012, Nobs had an accident while cross-country skiing and fell into a coma. He died on 10

January 2013; he was 76. The Museum of Montreux has described him as a "brilliant jack-of-all-trades". Nobs was succeeded as manager of the festival by Mathieu Jaton.

The rock band Queen first went to Montreux in July 1978 because of the festival. The band was formed in London in 1970 by Freddie Mercury, Brian May and Roger Taylor, and they were later joined by John Deacon. Mercury, the lead singer, was born Farrokh Bulsara in Zanzibar in 1946. His family moved to Feltham in England in 1964, not far from Heathrow Airport, where Mercury worked for a while as a baggage handler for British Airways. He met May and Taylor while studying for a degree. Queen decided to record the group's seventh album at the Mountain Studio in Montreux and gave it the title 'Jazz'. They bought the studio in 1979 and worked there on five further albums, including their last one 'Made in Heaven'.

Mercury composed his 1978 song 'Bicycle Race' after seeing the Tour de France pass through Montreux. He loved the peacefulness of the location (presumably when the festival wasn't taking place), and for a while he lived at the Duck House (Rue de Lac, 165) in Clarens. Later he bought a top floor apartment at the Territet end of the Montreux waterfront, and for the rest of his life he alternated between living there and in his Garden Lodge in Kensington in London. Mercury died at his London home in 1991, aged 45, from bronchial pneumonia due to Aids-related complications. After his death, the original Mountain Studio was converted into a museum, and a bronze statue of him was erected on the lakeside promenade in Montreux in 1996. Ever since 2003, around the end of August and the beginning of September, a special tribute is paid to him during what are known as 'Freddie celebration days'.

Mercury left his house in London and its contents to his friend Mary Austin, with whom he remained close even after he told her that he was gay. In September 2023, Austin decided to hold an auction at Sotheby's of 1,500 items from the house. A silver snake bangle that Mercury wore in the 'Bohemian Rhapsody' video was sold for £698,500; it had only been estimated to sell for up to £9,000. The auction raised £12.2 million, part of which was donated to the Elton John Aids Foundation.

Some of those who have performed at the Montreux Jazz Festival have also chosen to live in the area. David Bowie spent a few months on Lake Geneva in 1976, saying that the region inspired him to paint. In 1997, Phil Collins bought a house in Begnins (a small village between Nyon and Morges) which had been occupied since 1969 by Jackie Stewart, the Scottish Formula One racing driver, and his wife.

The music of the late American singer and dancer Michael Jackson has been heard on many occasions at the Montreux Jazz Festival. Jackson loved Switzerland, saying: "It's so clean and cool. We don't get much snow where I live, so I get real excited in Lausanne or Geneva. I'd like to buy a house there when I'm older and settle down. It's all so cute that it looks like a movie set." Sadly for him, Jackson never fulfilled that dream; he died in 2009 at the age of 50.

Shania Twain is a long-time resident of Lake Geneva who has entertained at the Montreux Jazz Festival on a number of occasions. She is a Canadian singer-songwriter who was born in 1965. Coming from a poor and dysfunctional family, she said:"I couldn't afford to go to a performing arts school, my education was in a bar". In 1993, Twain collaborated with and married the rock producer 'Mutt' Lange. In 1995, her second studio album ('The Woman in Me') sold over 20 million copies worldwide, and it was the first of three consecutive albums that sold at least ten million copies in the US. She has now sold over 100 million records and is the best-selling female artist in country music history, although the purists would argue that her music involves 'genre-blending'. One of her tracks, 'Man! I Feel Like a Woman', has been seen by the LGBTQ+ community as a celebration song.

Twain and Lange moved to Switzerland in the late 1990s and lived at La Tour-de-Peilz. However Lange was unfaithful, and after her divorce from him in 2010, she married a Nestle executive and settled in Corseaux, near Vevey. The new Golden Pass Express train, which started running from Montreux to Interlaken in the Bernese Oberland in December 2022, has been named 'Shania Twain' as a tribute to the star.

Chapter 5

Man's Humanity To Man And Nature

"Life's most persistent and urgent question is: 'What are you doing for others?'"
Martin Luther King, Jr.

In 2010, Shania Twain created the 'Shania Kids Can Charity Foundation' to help children fight poverty. Specifically, the charity is designed to create a programme in primary schools to assist children who fall into the gap between a dysfunctional home and qualifying for a social service intervention. Twain says: "These are children who may be experiencing abuse or neglect outside of school that may not be obvious, or children who are not necessarily being abused or neglected, but whose social and educational experience at school is affected due to personal issues which are out of their control." From 2019 to 2022, Twain had a residency at a Las Vegas theatre and took $1 from every ticket sold from her concerts and donated it to the cause; that raised over $150,000.

As mentioned earlier, the overriding principle of Switzerland's foreign policy is permanent neutrality. Another principle is solidarity, which has resulted in

Switzerland providing humanitarian aid to developing nations. The country will never get involved militarily in international conflicts and is not a signature to any offensive or defensive alliances. However, the third principle of Swiss foreign policy is availability, in that it offers to be a mediator in conflicts, and its principle of neutrality means that it stands a good chance of being trusted to fulfil that role. It also explains why Geneva has been chosen as the location for the headquarters of many international organisations, and as a conference centre. The American novelist Gertrude Stein wrote that "in peace times it is just Switzerland, but in wartime it is the only country in which everybody has confidence".

Before 1860, there were no organised army nursing systems for casualties, and no safe and protected institutions to accommodate and treat those who were wounded in battle. The Crimean War of 1854-6 resulted in the death of about 100,000 French soldiers, 25,000 British troops and up to a million Russians. At least two-thirds of the deaths were due to disease – to pneumonia, typhus, cholera and gangrene. The sufferings of the soldiers caused widespread condemnation, and the improvement of nursing and medical services brought about by the work of Florence Nightingale and others was the one lasting benefit of that war. In June 1859, the Genevan businessman Henry Dunant witnessed the aftermath of the Battle of Solferino in Italy, in which about

40,000 soldiers on both sides died or were left wounded on the battlefield. For a few days, Dunant helped with the treatment and care of the wounded, and when back in Geneva he publicised what he had seen, even writing a book about his experiences.

In February 1863, the Geneva Society for Public Welfare held a meeting, and by the end of the year the International Committee of the Red Cross (ICRC) had been formed in Geneva, where its headquarters remain to this day. It was confirmed by the first Geneva Convention in August 1864, a conference at which all European governments and the US, Brazil and Mexico were invited to attend. It is no coincidence that the Red Cross insignia is an inversion of the Swiss flag. Also based in Geneva is the League of Red Cross Societies, which is the parent organisation of 128 national societies, and whose main function is to co-ordinate aid during natural disasters. In 1867, Dunant was declared bankrupt; he had neglected his business interests while tirelessly pursuing his activities on behalf of the ICRC. These days, the Red Cross has around 97 million volunteers.

There have been three more Geneva Conventions – in 1949, 1977 and 2005. The 1949 conference formed the foundation of international humanitarian law. Then in 1977, two supplementary protocols represented an important step in adapting international rights during armed conflict to the conditions prevailing in modern warfare. The result of the 2005 conference was the adoption of an additional emblem known as the Red Crystal, the intention of which was to show the neutrality or medical purpose of those people displaying it in conflicts.

The World Health Organisation (WHO) is also based in Geneva. Established in April 1948, it is a specialised agency of the United Nations and is responsible for international public health. Its official mandate is to promote health and safety while helping the vulnerable worldwide. The WHO provides technical assistance to countries, sets international health standards, collects data on global health issues, publishes reports and statistics, and serves as a forum for scientific or policy discussions related to health. It defines health as a state of complete physical, mental and social well-being, not merely the absence of disease or infirmity. This requires that everyone should be able to obtain quality health care, and that includes access to abortion. It argues that when women with unwanted pregnancies face barriers to obtaining safe, timely and affordable terminations, they may resort to unsafe abortion.

The town of Morges saw the establishment of the World Wildlife Fund (WWF), a global non-government organisation which focuses on reducing the impact of human beings on the environment and preserving the wilderness. In April 1961, 16 of the world's leading conservationists signed the Morges Manifesto; they included the British ornithologist Sir Peter Scott and biologist Sir Julian Huxley. The document stated that while the expertise to protect places and species that were threatened by human development existed, the financial support to achieve this protection did not. It said that money was needed "to carry out mercy missions and to meet conservation emergencies, by buying land where wildlife treasures are threatened". The WWF opened its first office at the headquarters of the International Union for Conservation of Nature (IUCN) in Morges in September 1961, and Prince Bernhard of the Netherlands became its first president.

The WWF has been criticised for turning a blind eye to China's human rights abuses, and its persistent pollution, in exchange for being allowed offices in the country with most of the pandas in the world. The WWF's giant panda logo originated from an animal named Chi Chi, which had been transferred from Beijing Zoo to London Zoo in 1958. She was the only panda living in the western world at that time. Her easily recognisable features and status as an endangered species made her an ideal symbol that would overcome language barriers and be effective in black and white printing. The logo was designed by Sir Peter Scott from sketches by Gerald Watterson, a Scottish naturalist.

As the WWF grew during the 1970s, it began to expand its work to include conserving the environment as a whole.

In 1980, the IUCN and the WWF moved into shared new offices in the town of Gland, some 22 km (14 miles) to the south west of Morges. In 1986, the WWF changed its name to the World Wide Fund for Nature but kept the initials. It has now become the world's largest conservation organisation with over five million supporters globally and 1,300 environmental and conservation projects in more than 100 countries. The WWF gets more than half of its income from bequests and contributions from individuals, the rest coming from corporations and governments. In the 1990s, it updated its mission statement to include conserving the world's biological diversity and promoting the reduction of pollution and wasteful consumption. Meanwhile, the mission of the Tropiquarium de Servion, near Lausanne, is primarily to preserve endangered species. It is home to some little-known animals, such as multicoloured frogs, in flourishing vegetation.

When it comes to man's humanity, Nelson Mandela believed "there can be no keener revelation of a society's soul than the way it treats its children". The United Nations International Children's Emergency Fund (UNICEF) was established in 1946 to help children and young people whose lives and futures were at risk, regardless of what role their country had played in World War II. Nowadays UNICEF works in over 190 countries to save children's lives, to defend their rights, and to help them fulfil their potential. It is the world's largest provider of vaccines, and its work includes supporting child health and nutrition, safe water and sanitation, good education, and protecting children from violence and exploitation. UNICEF says it is non-political and impartial, but "never neutral when it comes to defending children's rights and safeguarding their lives and futures". Although its global headquarters are in New York, UNICEF has had connections to at least two famous people who used to reside near Lake Geneva.

Chapter 6

The UNICEF Connection

"I don't think we should judge celebrities for doing charity work. Whatever their reasons for doing it, they are shedding light on issues that would otherwise go unnoticed."

Liya Kebede, Ethiopian fashion model

UNICEF was one of the first organisations to enlist goodwill ambassadors, starting with the American actor and comedian Danny Kaye in 1954. Goodwill ambassadors volunteer their time to raise awareness and to help UNICEF reach the most disadvantaged youngsters with life-enhancing help and hope. As celebrities attract attention, they are well-placed to focus the world's eyes on the needs of children, not just in their own countries but by visiting field projects abroad. Ambassadors have included the actors Roger Moore, Liam Neeson, Susan Sarandon and Angelina Jolie, along with the singer-songwriter Katy Perry, footballers Leo Messi and David Beckham, and the tennis player Serena Williams. The two who lived close to Lake Geneva were Audrey Hepburn and Peter Ustinov.

Audrey Hepburn (originally Audrey Ruston) was born in Brussels in May 1929. Her father was an Anglo-Irish banker

Chapter 6 - The UNICEF Connection

who had been born in Austria-Hungary, and her mother was a Dutch aristocrat. In the mid-1930s, her parents flirted with fascism; her mother met Adolf Hitler and wrote favourable articles about him. Her parents separated in 1935 and were divorced in 1938.

In 1936, Audrey and her mother moved to the English village of Elham, south of Canterbury, where Audrey was educated at a small private school. She also attended dance lessons in an old hall in the village, and she gave her first public performance when the Elham brownie pack performed 'Humpty Dumpty'. However, when World War II was declared in 1939, Hepburn's mother and her daughter moved to Arnhem in the vain hope that, as in World War I, the Netherlands would remain neutral and be spared a German attack.

No longer was Hepburn's mother supporting fascism, especially after her brother-in-law was murdered by the Nazis in 1942. He was killed in retaliation for an act of sabotage by the resistance movement in which he had not been involved. After studying ballet, Audrey raised money for the Dutch resistance by giving silent dance performances. She also took food to downed flyers who were hiding in the woods in German-occupied territory near Arnhem. In 1943, when she was just 14, she noticed that one English flyer named Hector MacCourt had his family's gold signet ring with him. She warned him that the Germans would take it if he was captured, and she persuaded him to let her look after it until the war was over. He was captured, but in 1946 she kept her promise to return it, tracking him down to his home near Tonbridge in Kent.

Audrey Hepburn's career as a movie star spanned the years 1948 to 1989, although most of her films had been made by 1968. Some of her most famous parts were in 'Roman Holiday' (for which she won as Oscar), 'Breakfast at Tiffany's' and 'My Fair Lady'. In 1963, she became a resident of Tolochenaz, a small village just a short distance above Morges. After 1968 she largely retreated from her celebrity existence and spent many tranquil years near Lake Geneva; she lived in Tolochenaz for the rest of her life.

In the 1960s, Hepburn renewed contact with her father, after locating him in Dublin through the Red Cross. Although he remained emotionally detached, she supported him financially until his death. Hepburn was married twice. In 1954, she married actor Mel Ferrer in the chapel at Burgenstock above Lake Lucerne; they had one son but divorced in 1968. In 1969, she married Andrea Dotti, an Italian psychiatrist, in Morges. They also had one son, but Dotti had numerous affairs with younger women, and they were divorced in 1982.

Hepburn died in January 1993 from cancer of the appendix. On hearing of her death, one of her co-stars in 'Breakfast at Tiffany's', George Peppard, said that "a silver bell has been silenced". She was buried in a rather humble but well-kept grave in the small Tolochenaz cemetery among the less famous local residents.

Hepburn had been a UNICEF goodwill ambassador for the years 1988 to 1992. During that time, she made a combined total of more than 50 visits to Sudan, El Salvador, Vietnam, Ethiopia and Somalia. Her work for UNICEF also included visiting a polio vaccine project in Turkey and training programmes for women in Venezuela, initiatives for children living and working on the street in Ecuador, and projects to provide drinking water in Guatemala and Honduras.

Peter Ustinov (whose full name was Peter Alexander Freiherr von Ustinov) was born in London in April 1921. His father, who worked as a press officer at the German Embassy in London, was of Russian, German, Polish, Ethiopian and Jewish descent. His mother was a painter and ballet designer with French, German, Italian and Russian ancestry.

In his late teens, Ustinov trained as an actor and made his debut on the London stage in 1938. He later wrote: "I was not irresistibly drawn to the drama; it was an escape road from the dismal rat race of school". He appeared in 40 films and 14 plays, and he directed eight films (including 'Billy Budd'), eight plays and ten operas. His movies included 'Quo Vadis' (in which he played the Roman emperor Nero), 'Spartacus', 'Topkapi', and six films made between 1978 and 1988 in which he played Hercule Poirot, Agatha Christie's fictitious Belgian detective. He also wrote about 30 books, and then joked: "Books. I don't know what you see in them. I can understand a person reading them, but I can't see why people have to write them". There are of course numerous reasons why people write, such as to entertain, or to inform and educate. The British novelist George Orwell said he wrote "because there is some lie that I want to expose, some fact to which I want to draw attention, and my initial concern is to get a hearing".

In the 1960s, Ustinov became a Swiss resident and settled at Bursins, in the district of Nyon. He once told the British television presenter Russell Harty that "if you can see Lake Geneva from my house, you know it's going to rain, and if you can't see it, you know it is raining". He married three times and had four children.

From 1969 until his death, Ustinov's acting and writing took second place to his work for UNICEF, for which he was a vastly effective goodwill ambassador and fundraiser. In that role, he visited some of the neediest children in the world and made use of his ability to make people laugh. His travels on behalf of UNICEF took him to, among other countries, China, Russia, Myanmar, Cambodia, Kenya, Egypt and Thailand, and he lobbied governments at the highest levels to recognise the rights of children. He represented UNICEF in numerous international television specials over the years, and his inimitable style contributed to several award-winning radio and television commercials. On 31 October 1984, he was due to interview India's prime minister Indira Gandhi for Irish television, but she was assassinated on her way to the meeting.

Ustinov, who was knighted in 1990, was the president of the World Federalist Movement (WFM) from 1991 until his death from heart failure in March 2004. The WFM is a non-governmental organisation which was formed in 1947 in Montreux, convinced that mankind couldn't survive another world conflict and promoting the concept of global democratic institutions. Under its plan, the United Nations and other world agencies would become the institutions of a world federation. The WFM's founding Montreux Declaration said: "It is not between free enterprise and planned economy, nor between capitalism and communism, that the choice lies, but between federalism and power politics. We affirm that mankind can free itself forever from war only through the establishment of a world federal government." That will probably sound naive to most readers today, but in the shadow of the deadliest war in human history and the recent use of atomic weapons on Japan, it should be easy to understand why such an ideal might be espoused at that point in time.

Ustinov was buried in the cemetery at Bursins. He had

also been a secular humanist, and he once served on the advisory council of the British Humanist Association, where he argued that "the habit of religion is oppressive, an easy way out of thought".

Chapter 7

To Believe Or Not To Believe

"There is in every village a torch – the teacher: and an extinguisher – the clergyman."
Victor Hugo

Merchants and Roman soldiers spread the message of Christianity very quickly in Switzerland, and the first bishops were installed by the Church of Rome in Chur, Martigny and Geneva. With the Protestant Reformation of the 16th century, others were converted to an alternative version by the teachings of Huldrych Zwingli in Zurich and Jean Calvin in Geneva.

Calvin was born in Noyon in the north of France in July 1509. His father was a lawyer who worked for the local bishop, and his mother was very devout and took young Jean to pray before the statues of saints. Calvin studied theology and then law at the universities of Paris, Orleans and Bourges, and by 1532 he too was a qualified lawyer. He then underwent a profound religious experience, later writing that "God subdued my heart to docility by a sudden conversion". When reading the works of the Dutch theologian Desiderius Erasmus and the German priest Martin Luther, Calvin realised how far the teachings of the Church of Rome had digressed from the gospels.

After spending some time in Basel, which was a gathering place for intellectuals from all over Europe, Calvin published the first draft of his great work 'The Institutes of the Christian Religion'. This defined his theological position, declaring that the scriptures were the only source of guidance on matters of faith, and that salvation came through faith alone. It also argued that as faith was a gift from God, it was only given to those whom God had predestined for eternal life.

In 1535, the Protestant Reformation resulted in the Catholic priests being driven out of the Cathedrale St-Pierre in Geneva. In the following year Calvin arrived in the city, but his first attempt at a ministry there ended in failure. In 1538, he and two of his companions were ordered to leave within three days. As the bishop had only recently been driven out, there was no desire to allow a new ecclesiastical domination of the city. Nevertheless, when a cardinal tried to persuade the Genevans to return to the Church of Rome, it was Calvin who took up the cudgels to counter him. Soon there were growing demands in Geneva for his recall, and in 1541 he accepted the offer; his three years in exile had considerably strengthened his hand.

Calvin spent the rest of his life in Geneva. Although he claimed freedom from the Church of Rome, Calvin did not advocate toleration in religion, as he demonstrated when the Spanish theologian Michael Servetus arrived in the city in 1553. Calvin had him burned at the stake, principally for denying the divinity of Christ and for holding the view that the Trinity was "a three-headed monster".

Suffering from continuous ill-health, Calvin was frequently ill-tempered, and he was dogmatic and intolerant; no aspect of private or public behaviour was immune from his supervision. Although he never held any official position in Geneva other than preacher and professor of theology, he was the leading citizen, and by 1555 he was in complete control of the city. Geneva became very much like a theocracy, with Calvin as the prophet of God. It also became a cosmopolitan city, with Protestant refugees from all over Europe coming there. By the time of Calvin's death in 1564, the revolutionary impact of his doctrines was being felt throughout large parts of Europe, with literature printed in Geneva circulating widely. Geneva remained an independent and fiercely Protestant republic until it joined the Swiss Confederation in 1815.

Calvinism was the foundation of the Protestant movements in France, Scotland and the Netherlands, and in the colonies which Puritan settlers founded in the US in the 17th century. While in exile in Geneva in 1556, the theologian John Knox, who was a leading Protestant reformer in Scotland and the founder of the Presbyterian

Church, wrote that "Geneva is the most perfect school of Christ that ever was in the earth since the days of the apostles".

One of the distinguishing features of Calvin's ministry in Geneva was his belief in double predestination, an idea that originated with Augustine of Hippo in the fifth century. Calvin declared: "There could be no election without its opposite reprobation. Whom God passes by he reprobates, and that for no other cause but because he is pleased to exclude them from the inheritance which he predestines to his children." In other words, God not only determines which people are to be saved to Heaven, but he also actively chooses those who will be damned and sent to the other place.

The most obvious response to that doctrine is that if our fate has already been predetermined, what's the point of trying to be good? On the other hand, some people, such as the British evolutionary biologist Richard Dawkins, have asked: "Do we really need policing – whether by God or by each other – in order to stop us from behaving in a selfish and criminal manner?" Albert Einstein, the German theoretical physicist, argued that "there is one thing we do know; that man is here for the sake of other men – above all for those upon whose smiles and well-being our own happiness depends". He didn't think we needed God, or preoccupation with our eternal fate, as our reason to be good.

The Russian novelist Fyodor Dostoevsky (1821-1881) would have disagreed. In addition to some short stories, Dostoevsky wrote 13 novels, the most famous of which is probably 'Crime and Punishment', published in 1866. However, it was in 'The Brothers Karamazov', published in 1880, where one character contends that if you don't have faith in immortality, anything is allowed, and that leads to the murder of another. Presumably Dostoevsky thought that if belief in God suddenly vanished from the world, we would all become callous and selfish hedonists with nothing that would deserve to be called goodness. In the troubled political, social and spiritual atmosphere of 19th century Russia, Dostoevsky's writings analysed the pathological states of mind that lead to insanity, murder and suicide, and they explored the emotions of humiliation, self-destruction, tyrannical domination and murderous rage.

Dostoevsky, who suffered from epilepsy, had been a member of the Petrashevsky Circle, which had proposed social reforms in Russia and for which he was sentenced to death in 1849. He was spared at the last moment, while standing in front of a firing squad, an experience he used in his novel 'The Idiot'. He was released from a Siberian prison in 1854, but then had to do compulsory military service.

In February 1867, Dostoevsky married his second wife, who was 25 years his junior, and they moved to Geneva.

A year later they relocated to Vevey, where he worked on his novella 'The Gambler'. That story describes the bleak world of gambling with which he was all too familiar, having accrued substantial roulette debts. Dostoevsky and his wife then travelled to Italy, staying in Milan and Florence, before returning to Russia in 1871.

The Church of Rome did not cut much ice with the philosopher Jean-Jacques Rousseau. He wrote: "Man will never be free until the last king is strangled with the entrails of the last priest". He also pointed out that "the philosopher has never killed any priests, whereas the priest has killed a great many philosophers". Rousseau was born in Geneva in June 1712; the building in which he was born (40 Grand Rue) still exists. His mother died a few days after his birth, and so he was raised by his father, a clockmaker, who valued education and classical literature. Rousseau gained an apprenticeship as an engraver during his younger years, but he left his home in Geneva in 1728 and moved to nearby Annecy in France. He spent about ten years there as an engraver and music teacher,

Rousseau argued passionately for democracy, equality and liberty, and his writings represent an important contribution to the development of socialist thought. He incurred the anger of almost every ruler in Europe by loudly proclaiming and demanding the equality of man before the law. One of his main beliefs was the concept that humans are mostly good but society corrupts them, and much of his philosophy and his ideas stem from that. This tenet was thought to be in opposition to the Christian belief in 'original sin' (Adam and Eve eating 'forbidden fruit'), so it landed Rousseau in some trouble when he published such ideas. Yet five generations before Rousseau, his ancestor Didier, a bookseller who may have published Protestant tracts, had escaped persecution from French Catholics by fleeing to Geneva in 1549, where he became a wine merchant.

Rousseau moved to Paris in 1742 in an attempt to make it as a musician and composer. His novel 'La Nouvelle Heloise', published in 1761, is about a doomed love affair, conducted through letters, between a young aristocratic girl living in Vevey and her tutor; they were unable to marry because of the class difference. The story also features Lausanne, Clarens and Chillon.

In July 1778, Rousseau died in Ermenonville in France. A statue of him, made by the sculptor Jean-Jacques Pradier in Paris in 1834, was erected in Geneva in 1835 on Ile J.J. Rousseau, an island and park in the River Rhone which is connected to the shore by a bridge. Napoleon said "it would have been better for the peace of France if Rousseau had never existed".

Francois-Marie Arouet, born in 1694 and better known as Voltaire, died in the same year as Rousseau. He was a French satirist and philosopher who was banned from

Paris by Louis XV in 1754. He moved to Geneva, but then settled on the French side of the Franco-Swiss border after his relationship with the local Calvinists deteriorated. That wouldn't have been improved when he suggested that "those who can make you believe absurdities can make you commit atrocities".

Chapter 8

Scientific Connections

"The priests of the different religious sects dread the advance of science as witches do the approach of daylight."
Thomas Jefferson, third US president

Religious belief requires faith, while science requires proof. Religious fundamentalists believe that God made the world in six days, and that all species have remained unchanged since the time of their initial creation. Scientists believe in evolution, namely that all species have changed over time because of natural selection and genetic mutation. Scientific questions are framed in ways that can be confirmed or disproved by evidence; religious beliefs can just be based on faith and often involve supernatural entities. Yet there are people who try to have it both ways. A few years ago, a Church of England vicar was asked whether he believed in creation or evolution; his reply was "God created the world and then allowed it to evolve". Others have argued that while science is about the material world, religion has its moral discourse, and so there is a place for both of them.

If creationists find an apparent gap in current knowledge, they assume that God, by default, must fill it. It is hardly surprising therefore that over the centuries there has often been conflict between religion and science. One man who illustrated that conflict was Henri Nestle who, in 1875, pronounced: "There is no place for belief in modern science. What we do not know is a blank sheet which we must try to fill in".

Vevey was the birthplace of milk chocolate, primarily as a result of the work of Henri Nestle and Daniel Peter. Nestle was born in Frankfurt in Germany in August 1814, and after completing a four-year apprenticeship with a pharmacist, he went to work in Switzerland in the 1830s. That move was possibly precipitated by the political climate in Frankfurt, where committed liberals such as Nestle, and their families, were subjected to police surveillance. After Nestle's father died in 1838 and his mother died in the following year, he decided to settle in Vevey. He passed an exam in Lausanne in 1839 which authorised him to do chemical experiments, make up prescriptions and sell medicines, and he worked as an assistant to the pharmacist Marc Nicollier in Vevey for four years.

In 1843, Nestle bought into the production of rapeseeds, and soon became involved in the manufacture of nut oils, rum, absinthe and mustard. As his property in Vevey backed onto some large vineyards, he turned his hand to producing vinegar from poor quality wine. He even had a go at developing Portland cement, which had been patented by Joseph Aspdin in Wakefield in England in 1824. For a while, he also made and sold carbonated mineral water and lemonade, but in 1857 he switched his attention to producing gas lighting and fertilisers.

After 1861, Nestle worked on the research and development of infant cereal. Although he and his wife were childless, they were concerned about the very high infant mortality rate at that time. Nestle combined cow's milk with grain and sugar to manufacture a substitute for breast milk. Then he removed the acid and the starch in wheat flour because they were difficult for babies to digest. By 1867, he was working with doctors and scientists to develop the first complete baby food to be produced on a large scale. Nestle's powdered milk product provided the nutritional needs of young children, and it was soon being sold in much of Europe and the US.

In 1819, Francois-Louis Cailler, who was born in Vevey, had converted a former mill on the edge of the lake into the first chocolate factory, and he established the oldest Swiss chocolate brand still in existence. However, it was Cailler's son-in-law Daniel Peter, a neighbour of Nestle in Vevey, who is credited with inventing milk chocolate. Peter pioneered the process in 1857, which was cheaper to produce than dark chocolate because it had a lower cocoa content. He had a problem initially with removing the water from the milk, which caused mildew to form. Nevertheless, after receiving assistance from Nestle, who had invented a milk-condensation process, Peter was able to market his milk chocolate in 1875. He also pioneered the first milk chocolate drink, which was sold in triangular sachets consisting of powdered milk and cocoa to be added to water.

In 1874, Nestle became a naturalised Swiss citizen, and a few days later bought a home in Glion above Montreux for CHF 30,000. In 1875, he sold his company for one million Swiss francs and a two-horse carriage, which he wanted as a present for his wife. Under his successors, and particularly after the start of condensed milk production in 1878, the factory was extended. This meant that milk requirements increased dramatically, causing a shortage in Vevey, and so milk then had to be sourced from a wider area.

Nestle had a reputation for helping others with small loans and improving local infrastructure, particularly with regard to water supply. Soon after he settled in Glion, he provided the owner of the Hotel Righi Vaudois with a loan of CHF 125,000 so that he could expand the premises. Nestle died in Glion in July 1890. He was buried in what is now the small garden known as the Parc des Roses at Territet.

The manufacture of milk chocolate was further refined by Rodolphe Lindt, who in 1879 developed the conche, a machine which mixes and smoothes chocolate. He later sold his secret process to a Zurich-based company founded by David Sprungli; Lindt went on to merge with Sprungli in 1899. In 1898, the Cailler company opened a factory at Broc, where milk chocolate was soon produced on a large scale, and in 1901, Carl Russ-Suchard launched the Milka brand in Neuchatel. All Peter and Cailler brands were bought by the Nestle company in 1929, which eventually became one of the largest Europe-based confection industries. Julius Maggi invented the first instant soup in the world in 1886, along with the sauces for which his company became famous. In 1947, Maggi became yet another company to merge with Nestle, which has become the world's largest food and beverage company. It has around 275,000 employees and about 2,000 brands, and it trades in 188 countries, but its world headquarters is still in Vevey.

Apart from the invention of milk chocolate, the other great scientific development connected to Lake Geneva was the beginning of the World Wide Web at the European Organisation for Nuclear Research (Conseil Europeen pour la Recherche Nucleaire). CERN is located at the Esplanade des Particules in a north-western suburb of Geneva at the French-Swiss border. It is an intergovernmental organisation which was established in 1954 and has 23 member states. In March 1989, Tim Berners-Lee, a British computer scientist working at CERN, proposed a radical new way of linking and sharing information between researchers. He collaborated with Robert Cailliau, a Belgian informatics engineer, and the first website was activated in 1991. In April 1993, CERN announced that the World Wide Web would be free to anyone.

CERN is one of the world's most important laboratories, and in 2019 it had 2,660 scientific, technical and administrative staff members. It also hosts about 12,400 users from institutions in more than 70 countries. CERN strives to understand the universe through the study of fundamental particles. Before going any further, a few definitions might assist those of us, including the author, who weren't very good at physics at school. A particle is a minute portion of matter, the least possible amount. An atom is the smallest part of a substance that cannot be broken down chemically. Each atom has a nucleus (centre) made up of protons (positive particles) and neutrons (particles with no charge), while electrons (negative particles) move around the nucleus.

CERN's mission is "to perform world-class research in fundamental physics and provide a unique range of particle accelerator facilities that enable that research to take place in an environmentally responsible and sustainable way". It pushes the frontiers of science and technology, it trains scientists and technicians, and it tries to engage the public in the values of science. Visitors to

CERN will see scale models of the Large Hadron Collider (LHC).

The LHC was built 175 metres underground in the region between Geneva Airport and the nearby Jura Mountains. It consists of a giant ring-shaped tunnel which is 27 kilometres in circumference, with the majority of its length on the French side of the border. It smashes together protons and the other particles within an atom at close to the speed of light, in order to recreate the conditions that existed fractions of a second after the 'big bang' (when the universe expanded and stretched from being a single point to as large as it is now). These protons are accelerated in opposite directions and then guided by magnetic fields onto paths which see them collide at incredibly high energy. The particle debris can then reveal higher-energy particles that have formed in the collision.

The LHC, which is the world's largest collider, was used in the discovery of the Higgs boson in 2012, long after the particle was proposed by the British theoretical physicist Peter Higgs (1929-2024) and several other researchers in 1964. The Higgs theory of how particles acquire mass proposed a new kind of field that fills the entire universe, and the Higgs boson is a wave in that field. Its discovery, which won the Nobel Prize for Physics in 2013, confirmed the existence of the Higgs field.

Since the discovery of the Higgs boson, the LHC has not

revealed any significant new physics that might shed light on some of the deepest mysteries of the universe, such as the nature of dark matter or dark energy. In 2019, CERN drew up plans for the next machine, the Future Circular Collider (FCC), which would be at least three times bigger than the LHC. If the plans go ahead, the first stage could be built and ready in the 2040s for experiments which would collide electrons. The second stage, planned for the 2070s, would see protons slammed into one another. Anyone who finds much of that unfathomable is welcome to visit CERN and its science portal, where they can participate in such activities as quantum karaoke and quantum hockey!

Some physicists suspect that mysterious 'ghost' particles in the world around us could significantly advance our understanding of the universe, and in March 2024 CERN approved an experiment designed to find evidence for them. The new instrument will be about a thousand times more sensitive to such particles than previous devices, and it will smash particles into a hard surface to detect them, instead of against each other.

As science advances with such projects, the gaps in our knowledge shrink. Was Thomas Jefferson right? Could it ultimately mean that there will be nothing left to credit to God?

Chapter 9

Life, Death And Politics

"The simplest acts of kindness are by far more powerful than a thousand heads bowing in prayer."
Mahatma Gandhi

Gandhi (1869-1948), who led the non-violent struggle against British colonial rule in India, was born a Hindu, but had his own interpretation of the religion. Despite the growth in scientific knowledge, he thought there was still a place for God, and he also believed in religious tolerance and the oneness of humanity. He once remarked: "I am a Hindu, I am a Moslem, I am a Jew, I am a Christian, I am a Buddhist!" Gandhi welcomed contact with other religions, especially with Christian doctrines.

In December 1931, after attending a meeting in London on the future of India, Gandhi spent just five days in Switzerland, staying at the home of his friend Romain Rolland in Villeneuve. Yet despite the brief nature of his visit, there is now a statue of him and a square named after him in that small town at the eastern end of Lake Geneva. The statue, marking 150 years since Gandhi's birth, was a gift from the Indian government and was unveiled in 2019 by the Indian president Ram Nath Kovind.

Gandhi's head faces in the direction of the house where he stayed with Rolland. The plinth which forms the base of the statue is made of materials obtained from the Arvel quarry near Villeneuve.

During Gandhi's stay, which was the only occasion that he ever visited Switzerland, he delivered two public lectures, one in Lausanne and one in Geneva. However, the Swiss press was hostile to him, especially after he criticised several papers for the misrepresentation of speeches he had made in London. One Montreux newspaper suggested that the best thing Gandhi did in his five days in Switzerland was to get out. Rolland believed that the Swiss authorities would have forbidden another public meeting and might well have deported Gandhi had he stayed any longer. His anti-military and anti-capitalist comments made him quite a few enemies, especially when many people were still nervous about the spread of communism following the Russian Revolution of 1917. Gandhi also had plenty of enemies back in India. Beginning in 1934, there were six attempts to assassinate him, and the last one, in January 1948, was successful.

Romain Rolland (1866-1944) was a French novelist and dramatist who lived in Villeneuve between the two world wars. His most famous work, 'Jean-Christophe', written between 1904 and 1912, was one of the longest novels ever written, filling ten volumes; it won him the Nobel Prize for Literature in 1915. Rolland wrote a biography of

Gandhi, which was published in 1924, and like Gandhi he was deeply involved with pacifism, the struggle against fascism, and the search for world peace. He is noted for his correspondence with, and influence on, Sigmund Freud, the Austrian founder of psychoanalysis, and like Gandhi he was a vegetarian. Strangely, Rolland was also a supporter of the Russian tyrant Stalin, whom he considered to be the greatest man of his time. He even travelled to Moscow in 1935, where he had a meeting with Stalin, although he probably wasn't aware of all the evils which his hero was perpetrating; Stalin's great purge didn't occur until 1937.

Another famous Indian to visit Switzerland was Jawaharlal Nehru (1889-1964). He had been a prominent member of the Indian nationalist movement and became his country's first prime minister in 1950. Unlike Gandhi, Nehru was an atheist, saying that "the spectacle of organised religion has filled me with horror, and I have frequently condemned it". He went on: "Almost always it seemed to stand for blind belief and reaction, dogma and bigotry, superstition, exploitation, and the preservation of vested interests".

In June 1953, Nehru went to the Burgenstock Hotel to chair a conference of Indian ambassadors. After the conference was over, the English comic actor and filmmaker Charlie Chaplin was invited to spend some time with Nehru at the hotel. The meeting was arranged

Chapter 9 - Life, Death And Politics

by Louis Mountbatten's wife Edwina, who knew Chaplin and was rumoured to have had an affair with Nehru. Chaplin was collected from Lucerne railway station and taken by boat and funicular to Burgenstock. On meeting Nehru, Chaplin described him as "a man of moods, austere and sensitive, with an exceedingly alert and sensitive mind".

The two men got on so well that the persuasive Chaplin even managed to get the teetotaller Nehru to drink a glass of sherry. Nehru agreed to return with Chaplin to the house he had bought recently in Corsier-sur-Vevey. They were driven in the Indian ambassador's Cadillac, and they decided to take a shortcut through the mountains to save time. Unfortunately, the chauffeur drove recklessly along precipitous, narrow roads with sharp turns, had to brake suddenly to avoid a car travelling in the opposite direction, and skidded to a halt. The ambassador had been following them in a Chevrolet belonging to a former diplomat and almost collided with the Cadillac. There was nearly a pile-up in which both Nehru and Chaplin could have been killed. Luckily they reached Chaplin's villa safely, where they had lunch before Nehru went to Geneva for his flight home.

Charlie Chaplin was widely known for his silent movies, and especially for his 'tramp' character. He said that "all I need to make a comedy is a park, a policeman and a pretty girl". In September 1952, during the McCarthy era, he was banned from the US because he was suspected of having communist affiliations. However, an FBI file acknowledged his fame: "There are men and women in far corners of the world who have never heard of Jesus Christ, yet they know and love Charlie Chaplin". Born in 1889, he had a deprived childhood in Kennington, London, which probably shaped his political outlook as an adult. Later in life he said that "the saddest thing I can imagine is to get used to luxury". Chaplin denied being a communist but admitted to feeling "pretty pro-communist", and he was relaxed about the possibility that communism might spread all over the world. His sympathy for the working class defined his most famous silent films.

In 1931, Albert Einstein met Chaplin. Einstein said: "What I admire most about your art is its universality. You do not say a word, and yet the world understands you." Chaplin replied: "Your fame is even greater. The world admires you when no one understands you." Not everyone admired Chaplin; for example, the right-wing English novelist and poet Kingsley Amis described him as "a second-rate bicycle acrobat who should have kept his mouth shut".

In 1953, while on tour in Europe, Chaplin took a holiday in Switzerland, planning to stay for several weeks. He stayed for the rest of his life. He settled in Corsier-sur-Vevey at the Manoir de Ban with his fourth wife; he had married her in 1943, when he was 54 and she was 18. He did not return to the US until 1972, and that was only to receive an Oscar for Lifetime Achievement, where he told his audience "we're all amateurs, we don't live long enough to be anything else". However, he lived long enough to reach the age of 88 before dying on Christmas Day in 1977. Since 2016, tourists have been able to visit Chaplin's World at the Manoir de Ban, which has an interactive museum that retraces his life and work. There is a statue of him on the lakeside promenade in Vevey.

Another person with left-wing opinions who lived in Switzerland, but for a much shorter time, was Leon Gambetta (1838-1882). He was a lawyer who defended republican critics of Napoleon III, the last French monarch. He escaped from the siege of Paris in October 1870 in a balloon. In 1871, he left France and stayed in Clarens for a few months in self-imposed exile. He later returned to France and became the country's prime minister for 78 days spanning 1881-82, which was 28 days longer than Liz Truss lasted in that role in the UK in 2022. Gambetta was corpulent, suffered from poor health, and died from appendicitis at the age of 44. He is remembered as one of the founders of the French Third Republic, and there is hardly a town in France without a street bearing his name. That's something which will never be said in Britain about Liz Truss.

Lake Geneva has attracted those who were escaping persecution and probable death. One such person was Edmund Ludlow, an English parliamentarian and judge, born in about 1617, who is known for his 'Memoirs'. However, he is primarily remembered as one of those who signed the death warrant of the English king Charles I in January 1649. When the monarchy was restored in England in May 1660, Charles' son became king. Charles II is sometimes inappropriately referred to as 'the merry monarch', since his top priority was to take savage reprisals against all those associated with his father's death. Ludlow escaped to Dieppe in France in June 1660, from where he travelled to Geneva, Lausanne and Vevey. He was granted protection by the Swiss authorities in 1662, and he lived in Vevey until his death in 1692. A monument in Ludlow's memory, which was sponsored by his widow, is in the Eglise Saint-Martin in Vevey.

Andrew Broughton is buried in that church in Vevey. Apart from serving as the mayor of Maidstone in England, Broughton announced the death sentence at the end of the trial of Charles I. He escaped to Switzerland, arriving in Lausanne in 1662. He remained in exile for the rest of his life and died peacefully in Vevey in 1687.

Ludlow and Broughton died of natural causes, but Elisabeth of Bavaria (nicknamed 'Sisi') was not so fortunate. Born in Munich in December 1837, she married Emperor Franz Josef when she was 16. The wedding had been arranged between the emperor and her sister, but when he saw Sisi he demanded a swap. Sisi was unusually tall (1.73m, 5ft 8in) for that time, and was generally considered to be beautiful. On marriage in 1854 she became the Empress of Austria and, following the creation of the dual monarchy Austria-Hungary in 1867, the Queen Consort of Hungary.

Sisi was bullied by her mother-in-law, the Archduchess Sophie, who, as a result of the in-breeding which was prevalent in European monarchies until quite recently, was also her maternal aunt. When Sisi had her first baby in 1855, Sophie not only named the child after herself without consulting Sisi, but also took complete charge of the little girl. The formal Habsburg court life did not suit Sisi and she found it unpleasant. When she took up smoking, riding and gymnastics it caused much gossip. She suffered from ill-health for many years, and sobbed that although she loved her husband, she wished that he had not been an emperor. Tragedy hit Sisi in January 1889 when her son, Crown Prince Rudolf, died in a murder-suicide pact with his mistress. The incident has been the subject of various plays and films, in particular the 1968 movie 'Mayerling', starring Ava Gardner as Sisi, Omar Sharif as Rudolf and James Mason as Franz Josef.

Sisi liked to travel, and often did so without Franz Josef, but in 1893 they both visited Montreux and walked to Chillon. Sisi later stayed at the Grand Hotel de Territet and visited Lausanne and Geneva. Then in 1898, and despite warnings of possible assassination attempts, Sisi travelled incognito to Geneva, where she stayed at the Hotel Beau-Rivage. Unfortunately for her, an indiscretion by someone at the hotel revealed that the Empress of Austria was one of its guests, and that fact was reported in the local press the very next day.

An Italian anarchist named Luigi Luchini happened to be in Geneva at that time. He came from very humble origins and didn't like rich people, believing that all members of royal families were parasites. Luchini had planned to assassinate Prince Henri Philippe of Orleans, but he discovered that the prince had gone to the Valais region of Switzerland. When he read in a newspaper that Sisi was in Geneva, he decided to kill her instead. As she was walking from her hotel to catch a steamship to Montreux on 10 September 1898, Luchini stabbed her and she died soon afterwards. Sisi had been Empress of Austria for 44 years, longer than any other woman in that role. In the Parc des Roses in Territet, there has been a life-sized marble statue of Sisi since 1902.

Luchini was soon captured, but being aware that the death penalty had already been abolished in Geneva, he asked if he could be beheaded, thinking that would bring him even more publicity. He wanted to be moved to Lucerne, where they still had capital punishment, but his request was refused. He hanged himself in prison in 1910.

The Chinese revolutionary and politician Mao Zedong argued that "politics is war without bloodshed". The fate of Gandhi, Sisi, Charles I, and some of those who signed his death warrant, might suggest otherwise.

Chapter 10

War And Peace

"When it comes to peace and humanity, Geneva is an obvious epicentre."
Christian Bugnon, Helvet Magazine, Summer 2023

Mao Zedong also said that "war is politics with bloodshed", and few would argue with that. World War I (1914-18) resulted in 20 million deaths, about half of whom were civilians. World War II (1939-45) was the deadliest military conflict in history, leading to somewhere between 70 and 85 million deaths, which was at least 3% of the estimated global population of 2.3 billion in 1940.

Three years before World War I broke out, Italy declared war on the Ottoman Empire (Turkey). Other Western European countries had become involved in what was known as 'the scramble for Africa', and Italy wanted to gain some colonies in the north of the continent. The Italians soon occupied towns such as Tripoli and Benghazi, but they didn't manage to get beyond the coastal areas. However, in May 1912 Italian naval forces occupied some of the Dodecanese (literally 'twelve islands', including Rhodes, Kos and Patmos) off the Turkish coast. As Turkey was also having problems with the Balkan states within its empire, it sought peace, and the Treaty of Ouchy, also known as the first Treaty of Lausanne, was signed between Italy and Turkey in October 1912. Turkey conceded its rights over Tripoli and Cyrenaica (now known as Libya), and Italy agreed to evacuate the Dodecanese, although its forces continued to occupy some of the islands.

Following the end of World War I, a conference was held in Paris. The US president, Woodrow Wilson, attended with a list of 14 points for peace, arguing that "the world must be made safe for democracy". The first five points outlined general principles of peacemaking, none of which proved practicable or acceptable after 1918. The remaining nine points covered all the main territorial changes that seemed to be required for a stable settlement in Europe. Wilson wanted no more secret treaties, such as those which had helped to cause the war, no trade restrictions between countries, complete disarmament, and freedom of the seas for all ships. He thought that Russia should be free to choose its own form of government, that Belgium should be evacuated by foreign troops, and that Alsace and Lorraine should be returned to France.

Wilson was an idealist, and his original plan was for each nation to send representatives to a world parliament which could settle disputes between countries and alter the Versailles Treaty if necessary. However, Wilson's 14 points were disputed from the start, and most of them were ignored because too many of the delegates were more concerned with punishing Germany than establishing a new world order. Britain refused to accept freedom of the seas, only the defeated nations were disarmed, and trade barriers actually increased. British troops invaded Russia to help in a civil war against the Bolsheviks, and Italy demanded the land which it had been promised in a secret treaty. Nevertheless, Wilson's 14th point was accepted, and that resulted in the foundation of the League of Nations, the first ever worldwide intergovernmental organisation whose main mission was to maintain world peace. It aimed to prevent wars through collective security and disarmament, and to settle international disputes through negotiation and arbitration. The headquarters of the League was established in Geneva.

The peace conference decided that separate treaties would be made for each of the defeated countries. The Treaty of Versailles was signed on 28 June 1919 (the fifth anniversary of the assassination of Franz Ferdinand at Sarajevo, the immediate cause of World War I) and concerned Germany. The Treaty of Saint-Germain (10 September 1919) dealt with Austria, while the Treaty of Neuilly (27 November 1919) did likewise with Bulgaria. The Treaty of Trianon (4 June 1920) provided a settlement for Hungary.

The Treaty of Sevres (10 August 1920) abolished the

Ottoman Empire but was rejected by the new Turkish regime. Its replacement, the Treaty of Lausanne of 24 July 1923, was signed in the Chateau d'Ouchy (which is now a hotel and restaurant). When Italy's new fascist leader, Benito Mussolini, turned up at the conference, he made a formal announcement that he expected Italy to be treated as an equal, a request to which Britain and France agreed. The treaty was between Turkey on one side and Britain, France, Italy, Japan, Greece and Romania on the other. It dropped the plan to make Turkey pay reparations for the war, a penalty which had already been imposed on Germany but which was ended at the Lausanne Conference of 1932. The 1923 treaty recognised the boundaries of the modern state of Turkey, while Turkey made no claim to its former Arab provinces and recognised British possession of Cyprus and Italian possession of the Dodecanese. The treaty did not come into force until August 1924, meaning that the process of making peace lasted longer than the war itself.

The Montreux Convention, which was signed in July 1936 in the hotel now known as Fairmont Le Montreux Palace, was concerned with who should control the link between the Black Sea and the Mediterranean Sea. It was negotiated by representatives of Greece, Turkey, Britain, France and Russia. The convention guaranteed freedom of passage for all civilian vessels in peacetime, while limiting the movement of military vessels through the Bosporus and Dardanelles Straits in Turkey. It was agreed that in wartime, if Turkey was not involved in the conflict, warships of the nations at war would not be permitted to pass through the Straits, except when returning to base. Most of the terms of the convention are still followed.

When the League of Nations was set up, it was assumed that at least all European states would in future be democratic in structure, and therefore sufficiently similar and peace-loving to make the machinery of the League work effectively. Sadly, an increasing number of states ceased to be either democratic or peace-loving. At its height in 1934, the League of Nations had 58 member countries. However, it lacked its own armed force and was doomed to fail because the US Congress refused to allow the US, the most powerful country in the world, to join. Japan, Italy, Germany and Spain all left the League, and while the Soviet Union eventually became a member, it was expelled after it invaded Finland in 1939. The League proved incapable of preventing aggression by the likes of Hitler and Mussolini, the latter sneering that "the League is very well when sparrows shout, but no good at all when eagles fall out". Ultimately, the League failed to prevent World War II and was abolished in 1946. It was replaced by the United Nations, which has its headquarters in New York.

The Dodecanese became part of Greece in 1947. Cyprus achieved its independence from Britain in August 1960, but Turkey invaded and occupied the northern part of the island in July 1974. In November 1983, 'The Turkish Republic of Northern Cyprus', representing some 36% of the island, was unilaterally declared, and Cyprus remains partitioned to this day.

Chapter 11

From Russia With Love Stories

"If everyone fought for their own convictions there would be no war."
Leo Tolstoy

Anyone seeing the title of the previous chapter might have anticipated a connection to a very long novel set during the Napoleonic Wars. As Tolstoy stayed in Montreux for about two months, that story does have some relevance in this study.

Tolstoy was born in September 1828 into an aristocratic family in Russia. As his mother died when he was two years old, and his father died when he was nine, Tolstoy and his siblings were brought up by relatives. He went to Kazan University, where his teachers described him as "both unable and unwilling to learn". In 1847, he left the course in the middle of his studies, in theory to run the family estate at Yasnaya Polyana, 200 km (125 miles) south of Moscow. However, the reality was that he spent a lot of time in Moscow, Tula and St Petersburg, leading a slack and leisurely lifestyle and incurring heavy gambling debts.

In 1851, Tolstoy and his older brother went to the Caucasus and joined the army. In 1852, he started to write his first novel, 'Childhood', which was published in a popular Russian literary journal and was part of a trilogy (the other novels being 'Boyhood' and 'Youth'). In 1854, the Crimean War broke out, during which Tolstoy, as an active-duty soldier, witnessed some of the horrendous slaughter. He was promoted to second lieutenant because of his courage, but he left the army at the end of the war in 1856 and decided to travel around Europe.

In Paris, Tolstoy was horrified when he saw the public guillotining of a man, and that made him a lifelong opponent of the death penalty. By April 1857 he was lodging in Basset, at the western end of Montreux. He wrote in his diary: "It is literally impossible to tear oneself away from this lake and from these shores. I spend most of my time in gazing and in ecstasy, walking or merely standing at the window of my room."

While he was staying in Montreux, Tolstoy made several excursions to other parts of Switzerland, one of which was to walk to Meiringen in the Bernese Oberland, a distance of around 145 km (90 miles). His diary reveals that on the first day, he reached what is now the sleepy village of Les Avants, 5km (3 miles) on foot above Montreux and about 1,000 metres above sea level. When staying in Interlaken, he wrote in his diary: "I don't feel well. I woke up at seven. I walked to Boenigen. Beautiful, the women."

It's not clear as to whether he was writing about the view along Lake Brienz, which is indeed beautiful, or the ladies of that village, or maybe both. Not surprisingly, when he eventually completed his walk to Meiringen, he complained to his diary that "my feet hurt terribly".

Tolstoy was a pacifist, a vegetarian, and, despite his aristocratic status, claimed to be a believer in social justice. His experience in the army led him to write: "The whole military set-up is designed to change man, a good and rational being, into a wild and stupid animal". After returning to Yasnaya Polyana from his travels, Tolstoy married Sofia Behrs, the daughter of a physician, in September 1862; he was 34 and she was 18. They had 13 children, but five of them died before they reached the age of ten.

In 1869, 'War and Peace' was published. It is over 1,200 pages long and broadly focuses on Napoleon's invasion of Russia in 1812. It follows characters from diverse backgrounds – peasants and nobility, civilians and soldiers – as they struggle with the problems that were unique to their history and their culture. At the heart of the novel is a love triangle, involving two male friends and a young woman, a story which is filled with passion, misunderstanding and redemption. Characters in the story find peace and love during times of war and hardship. 'War and Peace' is known for its realism, something which Tolstoy achieved through intensive research, including visiting battlefields, while his dutiful wife copied out drafts of the novel for him several times!

'Anna Karenina', published in 1877, was Tolstoy's other great novel, and is considered by many to be one of the greatest works of literature ever written. It centres on an adulterous affair between a married woman and a young bachelor. When the husband discovers the relationship, his sole concern is for his public image, but eventually his wife becomes pregnant by her lover. The couple flee to Italy but then return to Russia, where Anna is socially ostracised but her lover is still accepted. Eventually Anna commits suicide by throwing herself under a train. Of course plenty of examples of such misogyny abound in the real world today. In the US, Kamala Harris has been criticised by some Republicans for being childless; just imagine what they might have said if, like Donald Trump, she had had five children by three different partners.

Tolstoy was an admirer of both Rousseau and his novel 'La Nouvelle Heloise', with its subject of a love affair which was unacceptable because it transgressed the class divide. The setting for that story may have been part of the reason why Tolstoy chose to visit Lake Geneva. His writings were also influenced by Dostoevsky, and both men deliberated on issues concerning God and immortality. Tolstoy's writing reflected on the questions that the inevitability of death poses for our understanding of life itself: if we must die, what is the point of living?

The death of Tolstoy was rather bizarre. With both him and Sofia losing some of their mental faculties, and after 48 years of marriage, the 82-year-old decided to leave his wife in the middle of the night. He was found sitting in a remote railway station, where he soon contracted pneumonia and died in November 1910. Tolstoy was buried near his estate at Yasnaya Polyana, which was nationalised by the Soviet government in 1921, and which is now a museum dedicated to his life and work. He is regarded by many as one of the best and most influential authors of all time.

The Russian-born novelist and poet Vladimir Nabokov, who was born in 1899, thought 'Anna Karenina' was "one of the greatest love stories in world literature". He was also influenced by Dostoevsky. Nabokov's family had been forced to flee from Russia after the Bolsheviks seized power in 1917, but despite his Russian roots, he liked to describe himself as being "as American as apple pie". He gained both fame and notoriety for writing 'Lolita' in 1955, which was one of the most controversial novels of the 20th century. It is about an adult man's passion for a 12-year-old girl, and it was clearly inspired by the true and tragic story of an American girl, Sally Horner, who was kidnapped by a convicted rapist in 1948. She was rescued after 21 months, but died in a car accident two years later, aged just 15. In 1980, the English rock band The Police released the song 'Don't Stand So Close To

Me'. It contained the verse: "It's no use, he sees her, he starts to shake and cough, just like the old man in that book by Nabokov".

In 1961, Nabokov and his wife Vera moved from the US to Lake Geneva, where they lived in the Fairmont Le Montreux Palace Hotel until his death in 1977. Nabokov described Montreux as "a rosy place for riparian exile", and he liked to stroll along the lakeside promenade with a notepad in his hand and some newspapers folded under his arm. Nabokov is buried in Clarens, and there is a bronze statue of him on the front lawn of that hotel where he lived in considerable comfort.

Apart from 'Lolita', Nabokov is also famous for 'Pale Fire', published in 1962, which is a satirical whodunit written as a 999-line poem. His longest novel, 'Ada', written in 1969, is another work with a dark side, telling the story of a man who has a lifelong love affair with his sister, believing they are cousins. His short story 'The Vane Sisters' is notable for its final paragraph, in which the first letters of each word spell out a message from beyond the grave.

Chapter 12

Anglo-American Literary Connections

"Writing and travel broaden your ass if not your mind; I like to write standing up."
Ernest Hemingway

Lake Geneva's 167 km (104 miles) shoreline is packed with literary associations, including a number of authors from the US and Britain. One of them was Henry James, who began life as an American and then acquired British citizenship in the last year of his life. James was born into a wealthy family in New York City in 1843. His family travelled around Europe when he was a teenager, which included a visit to Geneva. He was a shy but friendly young man who had a passion for reading books. His older brother William became a famous philosopher.

Henry James wrote stories, reviews and articles for a few years before attempting his first full-length novel, 'Watch and Ward', in 1871. He went on to write a total of 20 novels, including 'The American' (1877), 'Washington Square' (1881), 'The Bostonians' (1886), 'The Turn of the Screw' (1898), and 'The Wings of the Dove' (1902). In 1878, James made a visit to Chillon a pivotal episode in 'Daisy

Miller', a novella which first appeared as episodes in a magazine and then in book form in 1879. In the story, Daisy and her companion travel to Chillon by steamer from Vevey, a town which James describes as "seated upon the edge of a remarkably blue lake – a lake that it behoves every tourist to visit". He continues: "In this region, in the month of June, American travellers are extremely numerous; it may be said, indeed, that Vevey assumes at this period some of the characteristics of an American watering place". The story also makes reference to the Hotel Trois Couronnes in the town.

James lived at Lamb House in Rye in England from 1897 to 1914, and he died in London in 1916. He is considered by many to be one of the greatest novelists in the English language, and he was awarded the Order of Merit shortly before his death. James never married and avoided any serious involvement with other people. However, after his death it transpired that he had written what one of his relatives dismissed as "silly letters to young men". In 'Epistemology of the Closet', published in 1990, Eve Kosofsky Sedgwick suggests that James should be read as a gay writer whose efforts to remain in the closet gave him his style. Sedgwick believes that that may even have been his real subject, all the more present for being secret and submerged. 'Dearly Beloved Friends: Henry James's Letters to Younger Men', published in 2001, contains personal and sometimes intimate correspondence which James sent to four men.

There was nothing concealed about the sexuality of James' fellow American novelist Ernest Hemingway, who had four marriages (three of them to journalists) and three sons. Hemingway was born in Chicago in 1899, and he became an ambulance driver for the American Red Cross (a national affiliate of the International Red Cross) towards the end of World War I. He was injured on the Austro-Italian front in July 1918, was decorated for heroism and hospitalised in Milan, where he fell in love with a Red Cross nurse who turned down his offer of marriage.

In January 1922, Hemingway went to Switzerland for the first time, travelling from Paris to cover the final phase of the post-war peace conference in Lausanne for 'The Toronto Star'. He and his first wife stayed in Chamby, above Montreux, for four months, and he wrote several chapters of 'A Farewell to Arms' there. However, his first full novel was 'The Sun Also Rises', published in 1926. When Hemingway was resident in Paris in the 1920s, he used to spend the winter in Les Avants, where he soon became a proficient skier.

Hemingway converted to Catholicism in 1927 before getting married for the second time. However, he was indifferent to religion throughout his lifetime, despite a preoccupation with biblical themes in much of his work. The English writer Evelyn Waugh said in 1957 that Hemingway was "really at heart a Catholic author".

'A Farewell to Arms', published in 1929 and inspired by Hemingway's experiences in World War I, is arguably one of the greatest novels of that conflict. The two themes of the story are war and love, and they contrast the bitter feelings of a wounded American ambulance driver serving with the Italians with his passion for an English nurse called Catherine. The hero deserts the Italian army, thereby bidding farewell to arms as weapons. He and Catherine travel from Italy to Locarno in Switzerland by rowing along Lake Maggiore, before continuing to Montreux, where they live in a chalet on the side of a mountain above the town. Catherine becomes pregnant, and the story ends with the stillbirth of their son in a hospital in Lausanne. Catherine dies from multiple haemorrhages shortly afterwards, and the hero has to say farewell to the loving arms of his partner. The last four chapters of the story are set around Lake Geneva. The book was banned multiple times for sexual content and for its honest treatment of war; in the US, parents sometimes demanded that it be removed from school libraries.

Hemingway also wrote a novel which was set in the Spanish Civil War of 1936-9. The theme of 'For Whom the Bell Tolls', published in 1940, was that there's no such thing as a good war. In other words, there's no triumph in war that's not also accompanied by tragic loss and desolation in equal or greater measure. Hemingway was a keen fisherman, and his other works include 'The Old Man and the Sea', a novella composed in Cuba and published in 1952, the subject of which is an old fisherman who has caught nothing for 84 days. Two of his novels were published posthumously – 'Islands in the Stream' (1970) and 'The Garden of Eden' (1986).

Hemingway, who won the Nobel Prize for Literature in 1954, had a succinct and straightforward writing style, which was renowned for its direct staccato effect (short sentences written back-to-back). His work was noted for its 'intense masculinity' and tough and dry dialogue. In 'A Farewell to Arms', he shows how poignancy and horror can be increased by leaving out rather than piling on details; for example, the actual death of his partner is covered in half a sentence. Altogether he published seven novels, six short story collections and two non-fiction works.

Included in Hemingway's 1933 collection 'Winner Takes All' was a short story entitled 'Homage to Switzerland'. Once again autobiographically inspired, it is set in the station cafe at Territet and involves three different American men and local railway workers. One of the Americans offers the waitress a large sum of money to spend the night with him, but she refuses.

Hemingway committed suicide in July 1961. He shot himself in the head at his home in Idaho, just six days after being discharged from a clinic in Minnesota following treatment for severe depression and psychosis. Three years after his death, his fourth wife and widow published his memoir entitled 'A Moveable Feast'. In that he described how happy he had been living in a chalet just below Les Avants some 40 years earlier.

Another celebrity who was very familiar with Les Avants was the Englishman Noel Coward (1899-1973). Despite leaving school when he was only nine years old, he went on to become a playwright, composer, director, actor and singer, and he was famous for his wit and flamboyance. Coward published more than 50 plays, including 'Private Lives' (1930), which is a comedy about a divorced couple who happen to be honeymooning with their new spouses in the same hotel. 'Design for Living' (1932) is a comedy about the complicated relationship of three artistic characters. Coward also wrote the story behind the 1945 film 'Brief Encounter', starring Celia Johnson and Trevor Howard, which was remade in 1974 with Sophia Loren and Richard Burton in the leading roles.

At the beginning of World War II, Coward was in charge of the British propaganda office in Paris until the city was overrun by the Germans in June 1940. He received criticism in the British press for his foreign travels while people at home were suffering, but he was unable to reveal that he was acting on behalf of the secret service. Coward didn't make himself many friends when he said that he was "determined to travel through life first class".

That sentiment probably helped to precipitate Coward's decision to become a tax exile and leave Britain in 1956. He initially settled in Bermuda, but later bought houses in Jamaica and Switzerland, and he divided his time between these two homes for the rest of his life. At first he selected Celigny, a village near Geneva, to be his future Swiss residence, but as that end of the lake seemed expensive, he bought a ten-room chalet with four acres of land at Les Avants, where the Australian opera singer Joan Sutherland was one of his neighbours. He devoted a considerable amount of time to his hobby of painting, which is why he wasn't often seen in the village.

Coward, who was knighted in 1970, never married and was gay. He said that he liked long walks "especially when they are taken by people who annoy me". Coward was both a heavy smoker and drinker. He died at his home in Jamaica, but part of his collection of books was donated to the Montreux Museum.

Like Coward, the English journalist and novelist Graham Greene (born 1904) worked for British intelligence. Greene was recruited into MI6 by his sister in 1941, where Kim Philby, who would later be revealed as a Soviet agent, was his supervisor and became his friend. Greene resigned from MI6 in 1944. Like another of his friends, Charlie Chaplin, Greene had strong left-wing views. In 1957, he played a small role in helping Fidel Castro's revolutionaries overthrow the Batista regime in Cuba, transporting warm clothing to them when they were hiding in the hills. Greene met Castro on two occasions.

Greene had been born into the wealthy family which owned the Greene King brewery. He had an unhappy childhood, and he attempted suicide several times when he was at a boarding school; he was later diagnosed with bipolar disorder. In 1925, he wrote a book of poetry while he was still studying at Oxford, but it received poor reviews. After graduating, he became a war correspondent for 'The Times', which required him to travel extensively.

In 1929, Greene published his first novel, 'The Man Within', which was so popular that he was able to become a full-time writer. Over the next 60 years, he wrote numerous short stories and a total of 24 novels. They include 'Brighton Rock' (1938), 'The Power and the Glory' (1940), 'The Heart of the Matter' (1948), 'The Quiet American' (1955) and 'Our Man in Havana' (1958). His last novel was 'The Captain and the Enemy' (1988). In the preface to 'The Third Man' (1949), Greene admits that the story "was never written to be read but only to be seen", and the general consensus is that the film is better than the book.

Greene's daughter Caroline lived in the very small village of Jongny, on the hillside above Vevey, from 1973 onwards. He was inspired to write 'Doctor Fischer of Geneva or The Bomb Party' (1980) after playing pulling crackers with her at Christmas in 1979. The theme of this short novel is an exploration of how far the rich will go to debase themselves for more riches. Dr Fischer is a millionaire with a taste for sadism who despises the human race. He spends his time and money planning notorious parties designed to expose the shallowness and greed of his hangers-on. He challenges them to play Russian roulette with a 'bomb' and five cheques worth two million Swiss Francs hidden inside six crackers in a bran tub.

Like Hemingway, Greene, who had previously been an agnostic, converted to Catholicism in 1926 after meeting his future wife, Vivien, who was the world's leading expert on dolls' houses. However, in 1946 Greene began an affair with the wife of a wealthy farmer. The relationship is assumed to have inspired his novel 'The End of the Affair', which was published in 1951, after the liaison had ended. Greene had left his family in 1947, but his Catholic wife refused to give him a divorce, and they remained married until his death.

Greene was often referred to as a Catholic novelist, but he objected strongly to the term, preferring to be seen as a novelist who just happened to be a Catholic; he called himself a Catholic agnostic. Catholic novelists tend to see humanity struggling in a fallen world, and they create compelling characters who battle their demons and waver between vice and virtue. A Catholic novel may well have a theme which is directly related to some teaching or principle. Greene's work often did contain

Catholic themes, and 'Brighton Rock', 'The Power and the Glory', 'The Heart of the Matter' and 'The End of the Affair' are collectively known as 'The Catholic Novels'.

Hemingway and his fellow American novelist F. Scott Fitzgerald were part of the American Catholic literary movement of the 20th century. Fitzgerald, author of 'The Great Gatsby', stayed at the Hotel de la Paix in Lausanne in 1930, where an original poem and inscription by him can still be found in the hotel's guest book.

Greene believed that "if you are seeking the truth, champagne is better than a lie detector". Alcohol can certainly make people drop their guard and reveal more than perhaps they intended, but Greene's remark might provoke some people to suggest that he was a champagne socialist. Nevertheless, he is regarded by many as one of the leading novelists of the 20th century, and in 1986 he was awarded Britain's Order of Merit.

In the summer of 1990, Greene bought an apartment in Corseaux. Considering the amount of time he spent in the country, it is somewhat surprising that he once said "Switzerland is only bearable covered with snow, like some people are only bearable under a sheet". In 1991, Greene died in hospital in Vevey from leukemia, and he is buried in the cemetery at Corseaux.

Chapter 13

Medieval Connections

"We owe to the Middle Ages the two worst inventions of humanity – romantic love and gunpowder."
Andre Maurois, French author

The English novelist Mary Shelley (born 1797) wrote the Gothic novel 'Frankenstein' (or 'The Modern Prometheus'), which was published in 1818. She was the second wife of Percy Bysshe Shelley, an English poet who was born in Warnham in West Sussex in 1792; his first wife had committed suicide. Early chapters of the book, which is considered to be one of the first examples of science fiction, were drafted near Lake Geneva. Mary spent the summer of 1816 at a villa in Cologny, near Geneva, with her husband and a British writer and physician named John Polidori. They met up with Lord Byron, and they shared ghost stories and thought up new ideas. In 1818, the Shelleys moved to Italy, where Percy drowned in 1822 when his sailing boat sank. Mary died from a brain tumour in London in 1851.

Lord George Byron (born 1788) was an English poet, and he and Percy Shelley are seen as major figures of Romanticism, a concept which isn't easy to define. However, it is characterised by the celebration of the

Chapter 13 - Medieval Connections

powers of nature, glorifying individuality, infusing the spiritual and the supernatural, and rebellion against tradition. For example, Shelley attacked society's conservative elements (king, church and aristocracy) and looked to the future to bring a better world.

Byron was a reckless individual who racked up ever-increasing debts and married an heiress to a fortune in 1815, assuming that would restore him to solvency. However, he treated her badly and she left him after barely a year of marriage. The scandal of the separation, the strong likelihood that he had been involved in an incestuous relationship with his half-sister, plus his numerous debts, forced him to go abroad in April 1816 for his own safety. He never returned to England.

While he was staying at the Angleterre and Residence Hotel in Ouchy in 1816, Byron, along with Percy Shelley, made a tour of Lake Geneva. Their boatman told them the story of the prisoner of Chillon, Francois Bonivard, the prior of St Victor's Monastery in Geneva, who had been imprisoned there in the 16th century. Moved by the story, Byron visited Bonivard's cell in the castle, where you can still see Byron's name carved into a pillar. Back in his hotel, Byron scribbled out his 'Prisoner of Chillon', a long narrative poem supposedly spoken by Bonivard, but entirely fictitious. The poem celebrates the cause of individual liberty, and it brought Chillon to the attention of the wealthy tourists who were starting to explore the Alps. Shelley wrote of Chillon: "I have never seen a monument more frighteningly elevated by the insensible and inhuman tyranny which a man took delight in inflicting on a man".

Byron later fought in the Greek War of Independence against the Ottoman Turks. He was a bitter opponent of Lord Elgin's removal of the Parthenon marbles from Athens, and he denounced it in his poem 'The Curse of Minerva'. Byron died from a fever in 1824 while leading a campaign for the Greeks.

There is evidence that humans lived at Chillon in the Bronze Age, but the oldest historical document related to the castle shows that it belonged to the bishops of Sion. In those days it was just a collection of 25 small buildings crammed onto the rocky island, but over time those buildings merged and became part of the structure that is visible now. It was a stronghold of the House of Savoy from the 12th century until 1536. Transformed and enlarged in the 13th century, its location meant that its owners could charge tolls and control the import and export of goods on the transit road from Burgundy over the Great St Bernard Pass into Italy.

The House of Savoy was a royal dynasty which was established in 1003 in the Alpine region to the north-west of Italy. Over the years, it expanded its territory and influence through marriages and international diplomacy, eventually to include nearly all the Italian peninsula. In the 1530s, Savoy was ruled by Beatrice of Portugal, who was the sister-in-law of the Emperor Charles V. Her husband, the Duke of Savoy (also called Charles), was a weak man whose nickname 'Charles the Good' was a misnomer. His sole claim to fame was the manner of his death – he literally got out of bed on the wrong side – but ascertaining exactly how that led to his demise has proved elusive.

It was Charles who arranged for Francois Bonivard to be captured and taken to Chillon. Despite being a monk, Bonivard supported the Protestant reformers in Geneva, a move which wasn't well received by the local bishop. In addition, the people of Geneva were in conflict with Charles, and Bonivard was accused of inciting them to ally with the Bernese. For two years he was detained in reasonably 'comfortable' accommodation, but in 1532 he was shackled to a pillar in the dungeon. In 1536 he was freed when, after a three-year siege, the castle was captured by the Bernese.

As with the Savoys, the Bernese used Chillon as a weapons store and a prison. They held it until 1798 when the local people of Vaud, inspired by the French Revolution of 1789, took control of it. Rousseau set part of his novel 'La Nouvelle Heloise' in the castle, Writing about the fate of Bonivard, Victor Hugo described what he saw at Chillon: "He could only lie on the rock with a great deal of sorrows and without being able to spread his body parts". Chillon was the inspiration for the castle in the Walt Disney film 'The Little Mermaid', released in 1989.

The castle in Morges was built on the orders of Louis of Savoy, starting in 1286, and it was also captured by the Bernese in 1536. It became an arsenal for the canton of Vaud in 1803. Since 1932 it has housed the Vaud Military Museum, which occupies eleven of its rooms. The museum contains more than 10,000 objects, consisting of antique weapons, figurines, regulation firearms and uniforms dating from the early 16th century.

In April 1536, Beatrice fled from the French conquest of Savoy, and most of Charles III's lands were occupied and ruled by the French between 1536 and Charles' death in 1553. The Duchy of Savoy lasted until 1860 and included parts of what is now Western Italy and Lake Geneva.

The small medieval village of Yvoire, in the French section of the lake, was fortified by Amadeus V, who was the Count of Savoy between 1285 and 1323, and the chateau still dominates the small town. The village soon gained an important role in protecting the strategic trade routes through the Alps and along the lake. However, from the 16th century onwards, changing trade routes pushed Yvoire into decline and relative obscurity. Nevertheless, the mass tourism which developed in the 20th century put the village back on the map. Nowadays Yvoire is very popular with day-trippers from other parts of the lake, and it has a large number of restaurants, boutiques, art galleries and souvenir shops. It has received a national prize for its floral decoration and is a member of the Association of the Most Beautiful Villages of France. Between mid-April and early October, tourists can visit the Garden of Five Senses, which is inspired by the symbolism of medieval mazes. Yvoire can be reached in 20 minutes on a passenger ferry crossing from Nyon, and is only a short drive from Geneva or Evian.

Chapter 14

Take The Water Or The Wine

"I'm not a heavy drinker, I can sometimes go for hours without touching a drop."
Noel Coward

Evian is a holiday resort and spa on the French side of Lake Geneva, 35 minutes by passenger ferry from Ouchy across the widest part of the lake. It featured in Mary Shelley's novel 'Frankenstein'. A conference was held there in July 1938 to discuss the issue of Jewish refugees, and then German troops occupied the town during World War II. In March 1962, a set of peace treaties which recognised Algeria's independence from France were signed in the town.

Le Palais Lumiere in Evian, which dates from 1902, became a convention and cultural centre in 2006. However, Evian is most famous for giving its name to the water which is bottled there. It was Count Jean-Charles de Laizer in 1789 who was the first to claim that the water had health benefits. Laizer had fled from the French Revolution of that year, and he stayed in Evian until 1792. At that time Evian was in Savoy, which did not become part of France until the Treaty of Turin was signed in 1860. Laizer found lodgings in the home of Gabriel Cachat, whose garden had a spring of water. He drank some of the water every day, after which he claimed that his health improved, although maybe much of his 'illness' had just been the stress of escaping from a violent revolution?

There was no great awareness of the local springs at the time of the French Revolution, but Napoleon's regime had an interest in spa towns and inspired a scientist to analyse the Evian springs in 1807 and 1808. Cachat fenced off the spring and started charging a fee for the water, which a number of doctors prescribed. In 1823, a Genevan businessman started the Evian mineral water company and purchased the two main springs in the town, one of them being the Cachat spring. That company eventually went bankrupt, and the springs were bought by the Hotel des Bains, but in 1859 Evian became a public company.

Evian water is now owned by Danone, a French multinational corporation, and, despite being expensive, the water is exported to much of the world. Tourists can visit both the bottling plant, which is located between Evian and Thonon, and the original Cachat spring. Evian water is mentioned in the Agatha Christie story 'Murder on the Orient Express'. In January 2024, a New York judge ruled that the label on bottles of Evian water is wrong when it claims to be carbon neutral.

If expensive bottled water is not to your taste, you can sample the produce of the south-facing slopes on the Swiss side of the lake, where a somewhat stronger liquid is marketed. Grapes have been cultivated for winemaking in western and southern parts of Switzerland since the Roman empire of the first century BC, and 99 million bottles of wine (each 750ml) were produced in 2022. However, it is impossible for Swiss vineyards to provide enough wine to cover the country's needs; just about one-third of what is consumed each year originates in Switzerland. It is hardly surprising therefore that only about 1% of Swiss wine is exported, with imports of wine being much greater. The reason for that is because vines can only be cultivated in the most temperate regions of Switzerland, one of which is Lake Geneva. The lake is an important feature in the area's growing conditions, moderating both summer and winter temperatures and reflecting a great deal of light from the alpine water.

Most, but not all, Swiss wines come from five areas of the country: the Valais, Ticino, the shores of Lake Neuchatel, the canton of Vaud overlooking Lake Geneva, and the area north of the city of Geneva known as Mandement. About 26% of all Swiss wines are produced in Vaud. A further 9% emanate from the 1,400 hectares (3,500 acres) of vineyards and more than 95 wineries in Mandement, which is the source of many wines made from the Chasselas grape. In the 1980s, nearly 70% of

Swiss wines were white, but in the 21st century red wines have become more prevalent.

The canton of Vaud consists of three main areas. Firstly, there is La Cote, which is the western half of the lake's north shore between Geneva and Lausanne. Secondly, there is Lavaux, to the east of Lausanne, and thirdly there is Chablais, from the corner of the lake around Villeneuve and upstream into the valley of the Rhone. The area known as La Cote produces wines from Mont-sur-Rolle and Fechy. The slopes of the Lavaux district, bordering the lakefront east of Lausanne, are especially spectacular. The hillsides are so steep that they need extensive terracing (a practice started by Cistercian monks almost a thousand years ago), and the highest vineyards are 350 metres (1150 feet) above the lake. Most vine-growers here either sell their harvests under contract or join together in co-operative wineries, but some do make and sell their own wine. The area is the source of wines from Dezaley, Epesses, Cully and St Saphorin, but the Lavaux appellation also covers the vineyards to Montreux and further east, bordering Villeneuve. The red wines from this area are Pinot Noir and Gamay. The Lavaux vineyards have been a UNESCO World Heritage Site since 2007.

Ever since 1797, the town of Vevey has held its Fete des Vignerons (Winegrowers' Festival) every 20 to 25 years, the most recent occasions being in 1999 and 2019. It is a show which celebrates working on the land, the grape harvest and the world of winemaking. Performances take place in the Vevey market square, while other festivities are arranged around the town. July/August 2019 was the 12th time that this once in a generation show had been performed. Since 2016, it has been included in UNESCO's list of intangible cultural heritages. Mementos of the festival are an important feature of the Museum of the Brotherhood of Wine Growers in Vevey. That is located in a building dating from 1599 which was once the residence of the Bernese overlords when they ruled Vaud.

Vevey is also home to the Alimentarium, the first museum in the world entirely devoted to food and nutrition, which was opened in 1985. It was founded by Nestle in a listed building which used to be the company's management headquarters. It has workshops, demonstrations and lively animations. In its digital area, the museum provides expert fact sheets, in-depth articles, digitised objects, online courses, games and an educational platform. Its emblem is an eight-metre high fork which protrudes from the lake opposite the museum. Its permanent exhibition is structured around three sectors – Food, Society and the Body.

Chapter 15

A Healthy Body

"Sport is friendship, sport is health, sport is education, sport is life, sport brings the world together."
Juan Antonio Samaranch,
1996 Olympic Games Opening Ceremony

Pierre de Coubertin (1863-1937), a French baron and historian, believed that sport contributed to the harmonious and well-balanced development of the body, personality and mind. For a number of years, he advocated the inclusion of physical education in the curriculum of French high schools. Then de Coubertin heard about the Wenlock Olympian Society in Shropshire in England, which had been organising a local version of the Olympic Games annually since 1850. The society had been founded by a surgeon, William Penny Brookes, "for the moral, physical and intellectual improvement of the inhabitants of Wenlock", and it still functions today. Incidentally, the Wenlock Olympian Games of 1867 is thought to have been one of the first sports events ever to be photographed.

When de Coubertin visited Much Wenlock in 1890 he was impressed, later saying that "the Wenlock people alone have followed the true Olympian traditions". His visit gave him the inspiration to found the International Olympic Committee (IOC) in Paris in June 1894. Its aim was to help build a peaceful and better world by educating young people through sport, and specifically to revive the Olympic Games, which had ended in the year 393. The ancient games were always staged in Olympia in Greece, starting in 776 BC. They would have met with the approval of the ancient Greek physician Hippocrates, who said that "sport is a preserver of health".

The first Olympic Games of the modern era were held in 1896 in Athens. However, after that the event broke with the ancient tradition and was staged in places outside of Greece, although it did return to Athens in 2004. For example, in 1900 the Olympics were held in Paris, in 1904 in St Louis (Missouri), in 1908 in London, and in 1912 Stockholm was the host city. The 1916 Olympics were scheduled for Berlin, but had to be cancelled due to the outbreak of World War I, while the 1920 Olympics were held in Antwerp. In 1924, the Olympics returned to Paris, and the event later became the subject of 'Chariots of Fire'. That was a British Oscar-winning film, released in 1981, which focused on two of the runners, who were played by Ben Cross and Ian Charleson. 1924 was also the year of the first Winter Olympics, which took place in Chamonix in the French Alps.

Since 1915, the base of the IOC has been in Lausanne, which is now widely seen as the Olympic capital of the world. Lausanne is also home to the Olympic Museum, which was opened in 1993 in Ouchy on the initiative of Juan Antonio Samaranch, who at the time was president of the IOC. The museum was completely renovated in 2013, and its exhibition presents the origins of the Olympic Games, the competitions, and the athletic spirit through over 150 screens. The museum attracts more than 250,000 visitors a year and houses more than 10,000 artefacts, making it the largest archive of Olympic Games memorabilia in the world. The highlights include a display of Olympic torches, medals and shoes worn by competing athletes, and the museum even contains the boxing gloves of Pierre de Coubertin. The headquarters of the IOC are at Vidy, 3.5 km (2 miles) to the west of Ouchy.

Olympism is based on three fundamental values. Firstly, there is excellence, which requires constant improvement. Secondly, there is friendship, which involves accepting differences and diversity. Thirdly, there is respect, which calls for an uncompromisingly ethical approach to rules, to the environment, and to one's own body (such as by not using performance enhancing drugs). Since 1995, the IOC has worked to address environmental health concerns resulting from the hosting of the Olympic Games. Furthermore, it sees gender equality as a top priority, aiming to make access to both the Olympic Games and to sport in general easier for female athletes.

It also seeks to increase the number of women involved in sports administration and management. Regrettably, the Olympic Games have from time to time been subject to scandals and controversies, sometimes involving gender issues or the use of prohibited substances.

An original principle of the Olympics was that those taking part were amateurs, but gradually that requirement has been eroded. There was always the issue that, without remuneration, the opportunity to undertake the necessary and time-consuming training was largely limited to those with private means. However, some approved sponsorship has been allowed, and starting with the 2024 Olympic Games, gold medal winners are receiving prize money.

At the Beijing Olympics in 2008, the American swimmer Michael Phelps won a gold medal with a lead of 0.01 seconds, stressing the importance of very accurate timekeeping. Until at least 2032, the official Olympic Games timekeeper will be the Swiss company Omega.

Samaranch wanted Lausanne to become not only the administrative capital of the Olympics but also a city dedicated to sports for everyone, and it is now the home of numerous other sports federations. Since 1993 it has staged the Lausanne Marathon every year, usually in October, in support of young people in cancer remission in Switzerland. The course goes from Lausanne to Vevey and back again. In April, another long race, the Lausanne

20 km, is held. The Harmony Marathon for UNICEF has been staged in Geneva every May since 2005, apart from in 2020. It attracts around 9,000 participants, often from more than 100 countries, to take part in one of the eight races. These include a marathon, a half marathon, a 10 km race, a relay marathon, and a 20 km handbike and wheelchair race.

The Diamond League is an annual series of elite athletics competitions, consisting of 15 of the best invitational meetings. One of those is Athletissima Lausanne, a week-long international track and field meeting which has been held every summer since 1977. It is one of the biggest sporting events in the French-speaking part of Switzerland, attracting nearly 15,000 spectators and around 250 athletes.

Arturo Gander (1909-1981) was a Swiss artistic gymnast who was honoured in the International Gymnastics Hall of Fame in 1997. He became president of the International Gymnastics Federation, and every year the Memorial Arturo Gander is held in his memory. That is an international individual artistic gymnastic competition in which both male and female gymnasts can participate upon invitation; the location alternates between Chiasso and Morges. At the inaugural event in 1984, the Chinese gymnastic icon Li Ning won gold, just as he did three times at the Los Angeles Olympic Games of the same year.

After the Olympics, the most important international

sporting connection to Lake Geneva involves football. The headquarters of FIFA, the body which sets the overall rules and regulations for international football, and oversees competitions between nations across the world, is located in Zurich. However, UEFA (The Union of European Football Associations) has its own specific regulations for European competitions and has been administered from Nyon since 1995. UEFA was founded in Basel in 1954 at a meeting of representatives from 25 national football associations. It expanded considerably in the 1990s when new associations arose out of the fragmentation of the Soviet Union, Yugoslavia and Czechoslovakia. Its headquarters were originally in Paris, but were then in Bern from 1960 until 1995. UEFA has grown to become the umbrella organisation for 55 national football associations across Europe.

UEFA runs national and club competitions, including the UEFA European Championship, the UEFA Nations League, the UEFA Champions League, the Europa League and the Europa Conference League. It also stages the UEFA Super Cup, a match played annually by the winners of the Champions League and the Europa League. UEFA controls the prize money and regulations, as well as media rights to those competitions.

The objectives of UEFA include dealing with all questions relating to European football and promoting the game in a spirit of unity, solidarity, peace, understanding and fair play, without any discrimination on the basis of politics, race, religion or gender. It also aims to promote and protect ethical standards and good governance in European football, and to support and safeguard its member associations. They are indeed laudable aims, but to what extent has UEFA been successful in implementing them?

There are only 100 golf courses in the whole of Switzerland, partly because available land is scarce and expensive, but also because planning permission can be difficult to achieve. However, Montreux, Lavaux, Lausanne and Geneva all have 18-hole courses. Each September since the late 1990s, Geneva has held a golf tournament which raises funds for the Geneva Centre for Autism's life-changing programmes and services. Since 1994, and usually in July, the French section of Lake Geneva has hosted the Evian Championship at the Evian Resort Gold Club. It is a 72-hole tournament, and it is one of two major championships on the Ladies European Tour.

In July and August each year, a seven-hole street golf course is set up in Geneva. Each afternoon, clubs and foam golf balls are loaned out in the Parc des Bastions. The rules are that no more than seven swings are permitted per hole and passers-by have the right of way.

Every May, usually in the week before the Roland-Garros Grand Slam in Paris, a tennis tournament known as the Gonet Geneva Open is held in the Parc des Eaux-Vives, overlooking the lake. It involves more than 54 matches.

Since 1987, the Chateau de la Tour-de-Peilz has housed the Swiss Museum of Games. This is the only museum in Switzerland dedicated to the cultural history of games, and it now enjoys an international reputation. Its mission is to preserve and promote games from all eras and cultures, and to reveal the importance of games in the history of humanity. The museum contains a collection of more than 15,000 games throughout the ages and from every time and place, such as 2,500-year-old Egyptian dice, right through to the latest video games. The collections are based around five themes – educational games, strategic games, simulation games, games of skill and games of chance. Visitors are encouraged to play the games in all their forms, both inside the museum and in the castle gardens.

As mentioned in the first chapter, Lake Geneva is nearly 73 km (45 miles) long, and its maximum width is 13 km (8 miles). In August 1986, Alain Charmey from Vaud became the first person to swim the entire length of Lake Geneva. However, swimmers seeking a challenge are more likely to choose to cross the widest part of the lake, between Lausanne and Evian. The Guided Classique is a private swim arranged for individuals or groups, it is not a race.

It is hardly surprising that water plays a prominent role in the sporting activities of the area. The Societe Nautique de Geneve (SNG) was founded in 1872 and has been at

Port-Noir in Geneva since the early 1930s. The mid-1960s saw the rise of single-handed sailing, and the SNG is now the biggest yacht club in Europe, with more than 4,000 members. In 2003, Team Alinghi, run by Ernesto Bertarelli under the colours of the SNG, defeated Team New Zealand in the America's Cup.

Every June Lake Geneva witnesses the world's largest lake regatta, the Bol d'Or Mirabaud, which was launched in 1939 with 26 participants. It now attracts over 400 competitors, including some of the best sailors on the planet. The regatta has a 123km (77 miles) course, and it has become an established testing ground for new technological innovations.

George Orwell was no fan of organised sport. He saw it as a facet of nationalism on an international level and an expression of regional hatred domestically, while the American entrepreneur Ted Turner likened sport to "a war without the killing". The point is that sport isn't a war, and Switzerland, with its policy of permanent neutrality and a refusal to get involved in overseas conflicts, is an ideal country to administer non-lethal forms of international rivalry. Lake Geneva, with its strong connections to both the Olympics and UEFA, is particularly well-placed to provide 'the referee' for what is intended to be friendly combat.

Miscellaneous

From June to November 1846, the English novelist and social critic Charles Dickens lived in a villa in Lausanne with his wife, six children and his dog. He spent five of those months writing 'Dombey and Son'.

'The Ice Maiden', a fairy story by the Danish author Hans Christian Andersen, was published in 1861 and is set around a small island near Villeneuve.

David Urquhart, a Scottish diplomat and politician who introduced the Turkish bath to Britain, lived in Clarens from 1864 until his death in 1877 and is buried there.

The future British field marshal, Herbert Kitchener, was educated at a boarding school in Montreux in the 1860s.

The French artist Gustave Courbet, who died in La Tour-de-Peilz in 1877, painted 'Sunset on Lake Geneva' there and sculpted a fountain in the town.

Gustave Eiffel, who designed the tower for the Paris World Fair in 1889, bought a villa in Vevey and stayed in it for several months every year.

Ignacy Paderewski was a famous Polish pianist and statesman who bought a villa near Morges in 1898 and lived there for a while.

Paul Kruger, who was president of the Transvaal Republic

until the Boer War, lived his final year in self-imposed exile in Clarens after escaping from South Africa.

Elisee Reclus, a French writer and anarchist who produced a 19-volume geographical work, lived in Clarens from 1872.

Vladimir Ilyich Ulyanov (Lenin), who became the first leader of the Soviet Union, lived in Geneva for a total of four years between 1895 and 1908. He wrote for the communist newspaper 'Iskra' when it was based in the city.

The Irish inventor Louis Brennan was knocked down by a motor car in Montreux in December 1931 and died three weeks later.

Johannes van Laar, a Dutch chemist known for equations regarding chemical activity, died in Clarens in 1938.

Sydney Chaplin, an English actor and half-brother of Charlie Chaplin, was buried in Clarens in 1965.

Oskar Kokoschka was an Austrian artist and playwright who lived in Montreux from 1947 until his death in 1980.

James Mason was a British film star who lived in Lausanne for many years. He is buried in Corsier-sur-Vevey, close to the tomb of his friend Charlie Chaplin.

The Welsh actor Richard Burton and the Scottish novelist Alistair MacLean are buried in Celigny.

French-born choreographer Maurice Bejart developed a form of modern ballet in Lausanne, where he died in 2007 and has a metro station named after him.

The largest French-speaking comedy festival is held in Montreux every November, attracting international comedians.

The fictitious character Cully, in the long-running British TV series 'Midsomer Murders', was named after the village on Lake Geneva where she was conceived during her parents' honeymoon.

Didier Guzzoni, who was born in Geneva in 1970, is a Swiss computer scientist and founder member of Siri Inc, the company responsible for the Apple voice assistant.

New Zealand tennis player Lulu Sun was raised in Geneva from the age of five.

F. Scott Fitzgerald wrote that "Switzerland is a country where very few things begin, but many things end".

Bibliography

Automobile Association, 'Baedeker's Switzerland', Jarrold & Sons, Norwich, 1984

E.C.Belotti (ed), 'A Toute Vapeur, 150 Ans De La CGN', CGN, Lausanne, 2023

ed. C.Bugnon, 'Geneva', Helvet Magazine, Summer 2023 & Summer 2024

K.Cooper, Origins of the Universe', Icon Books, London, 2020

R.Dawkins, 'The God Delusion', Bantam Press, London, 2006

V.H.H.Green, 'Renaissance and Reformation', Arnold, London, 1964

A.Guignard, 'Chillon: The Prisoner of Chillon by Lord Byron', Grafiheld, Renens, 1989

E.Hemingway, 'A Farewell to Arms', Penguin Books, Harmondsworth, 1958

Kummerly & Frey, 'Switzerland 1984', Geographical Publishers, Berne, 1984

Kuoni, 'Switzerland & The Italian Lakes', JPM Publications, Lausanne, 2004

R.Lockyer, 'Habsburg and Bourbon Europe 1470-1720', Longmans, London, 1974

Roth & Sauter, 'Wines of Switzerland', Lausanne, 1973

L.E.Snellgrove, 'The Modern World Since 1870', Longmans, London, 1968

M.Swain, 'The Medway and the Military', Ingram Spark, Milton Keynes, 2022

D.Thomson, 'Europe Since Napoleon', Pelican, Harmondsworth, 1968

Online Sources

- https://www.weforum.org/agenda/2020/06/now-is-the-time-for-a-great-reset/
- https://www.project-syndicate.org/commentary/stakeholder-capitalism-new-metrics-by-klaus-schwab-2019-11
- https://en.wikipedia.org/wiki/Dublin
- https://en.wikipedia.org/wiki/International_Red_Cross_and_Red_Crescent_Movement
- https://en.wikipedia.org/wiki/CERN
- https://en.wikipedia.org/wiki/Clarens,_Switzerland
- https://en.wikipedia.org/wiki/Claude_Nobs
- https://en.wikipedia.org/wiki/Empress_Elisabeth_of_Austria
- https://en.wikipedia.org/wiki/Henri_Nestlé
- https://en.wikipedia.org/wiki/House_of_Savoy
- https://en.wikipedia.org/wiki/Igor_Stravinsky
- https://en.wikipedia.org/wiki/International_Committee_of_the_Red_Cross
- https://en.wikipedia.org/wiki/International_Olympic_Committee
- https://en.wikipedia.org/wiki/Lake_Geneva
- https://en.wikipedia.org/wiki/League_of_Nations

- https://en.wikipedia.org/wiki/Leo_Tolstoy
- https://en.wikipedia.org/wiki/Patek_Philippe
- https://en.wikipedia.org/wiki/Peter_Ustinov
- https://en.wikipedia.org/wiki/Pyotr_Ilyich_Tchaikovsky
- http://ibiblio.org/eldritch/hjj/dm/daisy1.html
- https://icytales.com/lake-geneva-25-interesting-facts/
- https://jwa.org/encyclopedia/article/haskil-clara
- https://living-with-rivers.com/en/the-incredible-story-of-the-tsunami-in-lake-geneva/
- https://olympics.com/ioc/beyond-the-games
- https://plato.stanford.edu/entries/rousseau/
- https://switzerlandisyours.com/E/celebrities/bios/84.html
- https://switzerlandisyours.com/E/celebrities/bios/85.html
- https://switzerlandisyours.com/E/celebrities/bios/89.html
- https://theculturetrip.com/europe/switzerland/articles/a-brief-history-of-switzerlands-beautiful-chillon-castle/
- https://theculturetrip.com/europe/switzerland/articles/how-switzerland-has-inspired-some-of-the-worlds-most-famous-writers/

- https://theswisswatchblog.com/2012/12/13/fun-facts-lake-geneva/
- https://thewire.in/external-affairs/charlie-chaplin-communism
- https://visit.cern/cern
- https://wenlock-olympian-society.org.uk/
- https://www.bbc.co.uk/news/entertainment-arts-65375583
- https://www.bbc.co.uk/news/science-environment-68631692
- https://www.britannica.com/biography/Henry-James-American-writer/Legacy
- https://www.englishclub.com/reading/environment/world-wildlife-fund.php
- https://www.exploring-castles.com/europe/switzerland/chillon_castle/
- https://www.freddie-tours.com/en/freddie-mercury-montreux
- https://www.greenleft.org.au/content/world-economic-forum-corporate-club-shapes-global-agenda
- https://www.hiddeneurope.eu/montreux-connections
- https://www.lake-geneva-switzerland.com/hautesavoy/yvoire/yvoire-medieval-floral-town-on-lake-geneva-france/

- https://www.latimes.com/archives/la-xpm-1986-10-05-tr-4419-story.html
- https://www.luxurytravelmag.com.au/article/in-the-footsteps-of-giants/
- https://www.montreuxjazzfestival.com/en/festival/about-montreux-jazz-festival/
- https://www.nestle.com/sites/default/files/asset-library/documents/about_us/henri-nestle-biography-en.pdf
- https://www.penguin.co.uk/articles/2019/10/where-to-start-reading-graham-greene
- https://www.rollingstone.com/music/music-news/claude-nobs-founder-of-montreux-jazz-festival-dead-at-76-203118/
- https://www.smoothradio.com/news/music/freddie-mercury-death-home-aids/
- https://www.swissinfo.ch/eng/culture/audrey-hepburn_swiss-sanctuary-of-a-very-fair-lady/12810
- https://www.swissinfo.ch/eng/culture/in-the-footsteps-of-tolstoy-in-switzerland/28829480
- https://www.swissinfo.ch/eng/multimedia/december-1931_when-gandhi-visited-switzerland/45225904
- https://www.swissinfo.ch/eng/society/dangerous-driving_when-chaplin-and-nehru-cheated-death-in-switzerland/45005666

- https://www.theguardian.com/books/2016/feb/20/colm-toibin-how-henry-james-family-tried-to-keep-him-in-the-closet
- https://www.theguardian.com/music/article/2024/aug/04/tchaikovsky-was-not-tragic-but-had-a-monty-python-sense-of-humour-says-biographer
- https://www.theguardian.com/music/2023/apr/26/freddie-mercury-collection-of-splendid-things-up-for-auction
- https://www.theguardian.com/music/2023/jan/23/shania-twain-childhood-stardom-divorce-survival
- https://www.theguardian.com/music/2023/sep/06/freddie-mercurys-garden-door-sells-for-over-400000-as-his-belongings-auctioned
- https://www.theguardian.com/science/2024/feb/05/cern-atom-smasher-unlock-secrets-universe-large-hadron-collider
- https://www.thehotelguru.com/en-eu/best-hotels-in/switzerland/lake-geneva
- https://www.uefa.com/insideuefa/
- https://www.weforum.org/about/world-economic-forum
- https://www.wine-searcher.com/regions-lavaux
- https://www.worldwildlife.org/about/history

Milton Keynes UK
Ingram Content Group UK Ltd.
UKHW021939311024
450473UK00012B/194

9 781805 416258